COOKING FOR 1 OR 2

Barbara Kyte
Katherine Greenberg

BRISTOL PUBLISHING ENTERPRISES
San Leandro, California

A Nitty Gritty® Cookbook

Printed in the United States of America.

ISBN 1-55867-089-0

Cover design: Frank Paredes
Front cover photography: John Benson
Food stylist: Suzanne Carreiro
Illustrator: Craig Torlucci, John Balkovek

CONTENTS

COOKING FOR 1 OR 2

Cooking for 1 or 2 can be as creative as cooking for a crowd. There are advantages to cooking in small quantities. Marketing and preparing meals are much simpler, and with fewer people to consider, it is easier to vary the menu, dinner hour and setting.

Our imaginative recipes are especially tailored to serve 1 or 2. Many have variations and helpful suggestions. They are nutritious, economical and easy to prepare.

We hope our ideas and recipes will excite you and that you will look forward to eating alone or with a companion.

PLANNING AND MARKETING

Our planning and marketing tips will help you eliminate leftovers, as well as unnecessary trips to the grocery store. Plan your weekly menu and make a shopping list, taking into account basic nutrition, seasonal foods and weekly specials.

TIPS

- When you anticipate having a busy schedule, plan one of our meals that can be prepared quickly, such as sandwiches or seafood, or make a pot of soup ahead to heat and serve.

- When shopping, avoid the temptation to buy foods not on your list. Buy only what you plan to use and have room to store.

- Don't shop when you are hungry! You'll buy more than if you were not.

- Ask your grocer to divide large packages of meat or produce into smaller portions. Or divide large cuts of meat or poultry into smaller portions at home to freeze for several meals.

- Purchase frozen chopped onions, green peppers, chives and lemon juice to have on hand.

- Plan to use perishable foods such as fish and berries within 1 or 2 days after shopping.

STORING FOODS

Proper food storage lengthens the time foods remain fresh. To prepare foods for refrigerator storage, place them in covered containers or wrap them in foil or plastic to preserve freshness and flavor. Before freezing foods, place them in airtight containers, leaving room for expansion, or wrap them tightly with foil or freezer wrap. Freeze foods in serving-sized portions. Most cooked foods may be frozen for up to 2 months.

- **BREAD:** Freeze what you do not plan to use within a few days.

- **DAIRY PRODUCTS:** Milk, eggs, sour cream and cottage cheese keep for 5 to 7 days in the refrigerator. They should never be frozen. Store cheese and butter in the refrigerator for up to 2 weeks.

- **FRUITS:** Ripen fruits at room temperature, and then refrigerate. Use ripe fruits within 3 days. Store apples and citrus fruits in the refrigerator for 1 week or more. Don't wash fruits until you are ready to use them.

- **MEAT AND POULTRY:** Refrigerate and use meat or poultry within 2 or 3 days after purchasing or freeze for up to 3 months.

- **STAPLES:** Refrigerate whole wheat flour, wheat germ, dried fruits and nuts. Store flour, sugar and honey, rice and pasta, cereals, herbs and spices at room temperature in sealed containers for up to 1 year in a cool, dark place. Other staples to have on hand are oil, vinegar, baking powder, baking soda, beef and chicken stock granules, salt, pepper and condiments.

- **VEGETABLES:** Store vegetables in the refrigerator for 5 to 7 days. Wash them just before you use them. Store onions and potatoes in a cool, dark place, but not together, and not in the refrigerator.

EQUIPPING YOUR KITCHEN

It is not necessary to equip your kitchen with every appliance and cooking utensil. Purchase only what you need. Small appliances and cookware are convenient. For best results, use small bowls and pans when cooking small quantities. Organize your kitchen so that items that are used together are stored together. For easy cleanup use disposable foil pans or line baking and broiling pans with foil.

COOKING

- 6 and/or 8-inch frying pan
- 10-inch frying pan with cover
- 1-quart saucepan with cover
- 2-quart saucepan with cover
- 3-quart saucepan with cover
- broiler pan with rack
- 1-quart casserole dish with cover
- vegetable steamer

MEASURING AND MIXING

- set of mixing bowls (stainless steel or glass are best)
- set of measuring cups (for both liquid and dry ingredients)
- measuring spoons
- rubber spatula
- wooden spoons
- wire whisk
- rolling pin

BAKING

- 2 custard cups
- two 10-oz. soufflé dishes
- 2 ramekins
- two 4-inch tart pans
- 8-inch round baking pan
- 8- and 9-inch square baking pans
- muffin pan
- baking sheet
- wire cooling rack
- pot holders

FOOD PREPARATION

- colander
- strainer
- spatula
- slotted spoon
- tongs

- ladle
- juicer
- grater
- peeler
- slicing knife

- paring knife
- skewers
- pepper grinder
- plastic storage containers

with covers
- cutting board
- can opener
- kitchen timer

APPLIANCES

- mixer

- blender

- toaster

OPTIONAL

- garlic press
- fondue pot and forks

- wok
- hibachi
- electric frying

pan
- toaster oven
- food processor

APPETIZERS

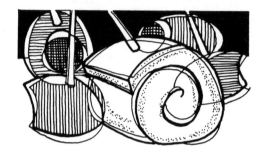

Appetizers set the stage for dinner. Select an appetizer that complements the meal you plan to serve. A light appetizer will stimulate your appetite before a hearty meal. For example, a fresh slice of cantaloupe wrapped in prosciutto is an ideal beginning for a dinner of *Minestrone Soup*, page 23, *Veal Piccata*, page 115 and *Baked Noodles Ricotta*, page 89. If appetites are light, the weather is warm or you just don't feel like cooking, choose one or more appetizers for a simple meal.

 # QUICK APPETIZERS

These appetizers are easy to make for 1 or 2 servings.

- Prepare an antipasto tray with an assortment of fresh or marinated vegetables, cheeses, olives and sliced meats.

- Wrap melon or papaya wedges with prosciutto.

- Wrap water chestnuts, chicken livers, shrimp or mushrooms with bacon and secure with a toothpick. Broil until bacon is crisp, turning once.

- Thread cubes of ham, cheese and cherry tomatoes or fresh fruit on a skewer.

- Top a 3 oz. package of cream cheese with chutney, or crab mixed with seafood cocktail sauce, and serve with crackers.

- Serve shrimp and raw vegetables with *Aioli Mayonnaise*, page 66, or *Salsa*, page 31.

- Marinate fresh mushrooms in *Vinaigrette* dressing, page 64. Serve with toothpicks.

HOT CRAB SPREAD

Makes: 2/3 cup

This seafood spread makes an elegant hors d'oeuvre for a special occasion. Serve with crackers or baguette rounds.

1 pkg. (3 oz.) cream cheese
2 tbs. white wine, optional
1/2 tsp. Dijon mustard
dash salt and pepper
1/2 cup cooked, flaked crab

Combine all ingredients except crab, and warm slowly in a saucepan. Stir in crab and heat through. Serve hot with crackers or bread rounds.

BOURSIN

Makes: ½ cup

This garlic- and herb-flavored cheese spread keeps for several weeks in the refrigerator.

1 pkg. (3 oz.) cream cheese, softened
2 tbs. sour cream
½ clove garlic, crushed
1 tbs. finely chopped green onions
1 tbs. finely chopped parsley
¼ tsp. dried thyme, tarragon or dill
½ tsp. grated lemon peel, optional
freshly ground pepper

Mix all ingredients together until smooth, using a mixer or food processor. Spread on crackers or stuff raw mushroom caps or cherry tomatoes with cheese mixture.

CHEESE BALL

Makes: 1 small ball

This hors d'oeuvre may be made several days ahead. It keeps well for up to 2 weeks in the refrigerator. Arrange slices of green and red apples around the cheese ball for an attractive cheese board.

1 pkg. (3 oz.) cream cheese, softened
½ cup grated cheddar cheese
1 tbs. dry sherry or brandy, optional
dash Worcestershire sauce
dash garlic powder
chopped nuts

Combine all ingredients except nuts in a mixing bowl or the work bowl of a food processor. Beat or process until smooth. Form into a ball and roll in chopped nuts. Wrap in plastic and refrigerate.

GUACAMOLE

Makes: ¾ cup

Not being able to obtain ripe fruits or vegetables from the market can be discouraging. Here's a tip to quicken the ripening of avocados: put them in a brown paper bag for a few days.

1 ripe avocado, mashed
1 green onion, sliced
1 tbs. lemon juice
2 tbs. chopped, seeded tomato
dash Tabasco Sauce
salt and pepper

Mix all ingredients together. Do not puree in a blender or food processor. Mixture should be slightly lumpy. Serve with tortilla chips.

HINT
Top tacos, burritos and enchiladas with *Guacamole*.

PATÉ

Makes: ¾ cup

Serve with crackers or French bread. Makes a good sandwich spread, too.

1 tbs. butter
½ clove garlic, chopped
1 tbs. chopped onion
¼ lb. chicken livers
2 tbs. dry sherry, optional
salt and pepper

In a small skillet, melt butter over medium heat. Add garlic, onion and chicken livers. Reduce heat to low and simmer for 10 minutes. Pour contents of skillet into a blender or food processor. Add sherry, salt and pepper. Blend or process until smooth. Pour into a container and refrigerate for at least 2 hours. Keeps well for up to a week in the refrigerator.

 # QUESADILLAS

Quesadillas can be served in place of sandwiches for a lunch or supper.

	FOR 1	FOR 2
oil	½ tsp.	1 tsp.
flour tortillas, 8 inch	1	2
shredded cheddar or Monterey Jack cheese	½ cup	1 cup
chopped tomato	⅓ cup	⅔ cup
diced green chiles	2 tbs.	¼ cup
Guacamole, page 12, optional		

Brush pan with oil and heat. Place tortilla in pan and heat on one side. Turn tortilla over and sprinkle with cheese, tomato and chile pepper. Cook until cheese melts. Remove tortilla to plate. Top with *Guacamole* if desired. Fold in half, cut into quarters and serve hot.

VARIATIONS

	FOR 1	FOR 2
sliced green onions	2 tbs.	¼ cup
chopped green bell pepper	2 tbs.	¼ cup
sliced black olives	2 tbs.	¼ cup
sour cream	3 tbs.	⅓ cup
salsa	3 tbs.	⅓ cup
refried beans	2 tbs.	¼ cup
sliced or slivered chicken, turkey, ham or beef		
crabmeat or shrimp		

SHRIMP ON ARTICHOKE LEAVES

Servings: 1 or 2

This appetizer makes a lovely presentation, and tastes wonderful, too.

1 artichoke
1 tbs. lemon juice
½ cup water
¼ cup mayonnaise

1 tsp. Dijon mustard or ¼ tsp. curry
  powder
⅓ cup small cooked shrimp

Wash artichoke and remove small outer leaves from bottom of artichoke. Cut off stem so artichoke will stand upright and remove thorny tips of leaves with scissors. Brush cut edges with lemon juice to prevent darkening. Place in a small saucepan and pour ½ cup water in bottom of pan. Cover and simmer 45 to 60 minutes or until leaves pull off easily. Add water if necessary. Or, place in a small baking dish and cover with vented plastic wrap. Microwave on high for 4 to 5 minutes or until done. Cool. Remove leaves from artichoke and arrange attractively on a plate. Stir mayonnaise and mustard or curry powder together to blend. Spoon a small dollop of mayonnaise onto the tip of each leaf and top with a shrimp.

SOUPS AND SAUCES

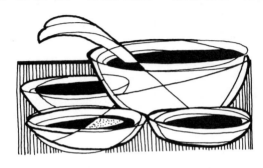

With the addition of delicious warm bread, freshly baked muffins or hot cheese bread and a salad, soup becomes a complete meal. Many of our soups can be served either hot or cold, providing you with more variety. Since it's just as easy to make a large pot of soup as it is a small amount, why not double or triple the recipe? The extra portions can be refrigerated for several days to be enjoyed later in the week. The flavor will probably be even better and you won't have to cook that night. Most soups and sauces also freeze well.

We've included a series of classic sauces, among them *Hollandaise* and *Sweet and Sour*, that will enhance vegetable and meat dishes and greatly expand your recipe repertoire.

CREAM OF VEGETABLE SOUP

Makes: 1¼ cups

Choose one of these light and nutritious soups to start a meal or accompany a sandwich. They are equally delicious served cold.

SOUP BASE

½ cup chicken broth
1 tbs. chopped onion

⅓ cup milk or light cream
salt and pepper

VARIATIONS

- **CREAM OF BROCCOLI SOUP:**
  Add 2 cups chopped broccoli and a dash of cayenne pepper.

- **CREAM OF CARROT SOUP:**
  Add 1 cup peeled and sliced carrots and a dash of nutmeg.

- **CREAM OF POTATO SOUP:**
  Add 1 cup peeled and cubed potatoes and 1 tsp. chopped parsley.

Combine chicken broth, onion, vegetable and seasonings in a saucepan. Bring to a boil. Reduce heat, cover and simmer 10 to 15 minutes, or until vegetable is tender. Pour into a blender or food processor. Add cream and blend until smooth. Serve hot or cold.

ZUCCHINI SOUP

Makes: 3 cups

This is a great way to use a bountiful zucchini harvest.

4 cups sliced zucchini
¼ cup chopped onion
1 clove garlic, chopped
½ cup beef broth
¼ tsp. basil
salt and pepper
1 slice bacon, cooked and crumbled, optional
grated Parmesan cheese

Combine all ingredients except Parmesan cheese in a saucepan. Simmer about 20 minutes, or until zucchini is tender. Puree in a blender or food processor. Sprinkle with Parmesan cheese and serve hot.

LENTIL AND SAUSAGE SOUP

Makes: 1 quart

This hearty soup is even better the second day. Serve it with French bread and a crisp green salad.

½ cup dried lentils
3 cups beef broth
½ cup sliced leeks or onions
½ cup sliced carrots
¼ cup sliced celery
½ cup grated potato

1 cup sliced garlic sausage
1 bay leaf
1 tsp. wine vinegar
dash thyme
salt and pepper
3 tbs. finely chopped parsley, optional

Combine lentils and beef broth in a saucepan. Bring to a boil. Add remaining ingredients and simmer covered for 1 hour, or until lentils are tender. Remove bay leaf and serve hot. If desired, garnish with parsley.

FRENCH ONION SOUP

Servings: 2

Serve this classic, robust soup with salad for a light supper.

1 tbs. butter
1 medium onion, sliced
2½ cups beef broth
salt and pepper
2 slices toasted French bread
¼ cup grated Gruyère or Swiss cheese

Melt butter in a small saucepan over medium heat. Add sliced onion and sauté until tender and golden brown. Add broth and simmer 15 minutes. Season with salt and pepper. Place toast in 2 heat-proof soup bowls and pour soup over toast. Sprinkle with cheese. Place under broiler for a few minutes until cheese melts.

MINESTRONE

Makes: 1 quart

*Top this nutritious vegetable soup with a spoonful of our **Pesto**, on page 85, and serve with French bread.*

2 cups chicken broth
1 small zucchini, sliced
1 cup frozen mixed vegetables
1 tomato, peeled and chopped
2 tbs. chopped onion
1 clove garlic, chopped

⅓ cup uncooked macaroni
1 can (8¾ oz.) kidney beans, drained
¼ tsp. oregano
¼ tsp. basil
grated Parmesan cheese

Bring broth to a boil in a saucepan. Add remaining ingredients, except Parmesan cheese. Reduce heat and simmer 15 minutes. Pour into serving bowls. Sprinkle with Parmesan cheese and serve.

MANHATTAN CLAM CHOWDER

Makes: 1 quart

Keep these ingredients on hand for a quick meal.

2 tbs. chopped onion
¼ cup sliced celery, optional
1 can (6½ oz.) minced clams, undrained
1 can (16 oz.) peeled tomatoes, chopped with juice
1 small potato, cubed
1 small carrot, chopped
dash thyme
salt and pepper
1 slice bacon, cooked and crumbled, optional
oyster crackers, optional

Combine all ingredients except crackers in a saucepan. Simmer covered for 30 minutes, or until vegetables are tender. If desired, serve with oyster crackers.

GAZPACHO

Makes: 2½ cups

A cold Spanish soup is perfect for a hot summer day.

1 tomato, peeled and quartered
1 can (12 oz.) tomato juice
2 tbs. chopped green bell pepper
2 tbs. chopped onion
½ cup chopped cucumber
1 clove garlic, minced
1 tbs. oil
1 tbs. wine vinegar
salt and pepper

Combine all ingredients in a blender or food processor. Blend or process just until vegetables are pureed. Chill several hours or overnight.

HOLLANDAISE SAUCE

Makes: ¾ cup

Serve this easy version of a classic sauce with asparagus, broccoli or new potatoes.

2 egg yolks
1 tbs. hot water
1 tbs. lemon juice
dash nutmeg or cayenne pepper
dash salt
½ cup hot melted butter

Run hot water over the blender container to warm it. Blend egg yolks, water, lemon juice and seasonings. Slowly pour in melted butter, blending until thickened. Serve at once. Refrigerate extra sauce and bring to room temperature before serving.

BEARNAISE SAUCE

Makes: ⅓ cup

This sauce is an elegant accompaniment to steak or salmon.

2 tsp. tarragon vinegar
1 tsp. chopped shallots or green onions
dash tarragon
⅓ cup *Hollandaise Sauce,* page 26

Bring vinegar, shallots and tarragon to a boil in a small saucepan. Stir into *Hollandaise Sauce* to blend.

SWEET AND SOUR SAUCE

Makes: 1¼ cups

This sauce is great on fresh, steamed vegetables; or use it as the basis for an entrée (see hint below).

2 tsp. cornstarch
1 tbs. firmly packed brown sugar
1 can (8 oz.) pineapple chunks
¼ cup water

1 tbs. vinegar
1 tsp. soy sauce
1 tbs. chopped green bell pepper

Combine cornstarch, sugar and juice from pineapple chunks in a saucepan. Stir in water, vinegar and soy sauce. Cook over medium heat, stirring constantly, until thickened. Add pineapple chunks and green pepper. Heat to serving temperature.

HINT

For a complete meal, add 1½ cups cubed, cooked pork or chicken, cooked shrimp or cooked meatballs, page 100, to sauce. Heat and serve over cooked rice.

BARBECUE SAUCE

Makes: 1 cup

A savory sauce, this is good for basting spareribs or chicken either in the oven or on the barbecue.

1 cup *Tomato Sauce*, page 30
1 tbs. lemon juice or vinegar
1 tbs. molasses or firmly packed brown sugar
1 tbs. minced onion
½ tsp. Worcestershire sauce
¼ tsp. chili powder
salt and pepper

Combine all ingredients in a saucepan and simmer 5 minutes.

TOMATO SAUCE

Makes: 1 cup

Homemade tomato sauce has so much more flavor than canned, and takes only 15 minutes to prepare. Fresh basil will add even more flavor to the sauce.

1 tbs. olive oil
2 tbs. chopped onion

1 cup peeled, seeded and chopped
   tomatoes (about 3 medium)
salt and pepper

Heat olive oil to medium-hot in a saucepan. Add onion and sauté until tender. Add tomatoes, salt and pepper. Simmer 10 minutes. If desired, puree in a blender or food processor.

VARIATIONS

- Add ¼ tsp. basil or oregano before simmering.
- Add ½ clove garlic, crushed before simmering.
- Add 2 tbs. chopped green bell pepper and sauté with onion.

SALSA

Makes: ½ cup

Here's a zesty sauce for tacos, steaks, or chicken.

1 medium tomato, peeled, seeded and chopped
1 tbs. sliced green onion
⅛ tsp. oregano
1 tsp. vinegar
2 tsp. oil
1 tbs. chopped green chiles or ripe olives
dash Tabasco Sauce, optional
dash salt

Mix all ingredients. Keeps for several days in the refrigerator.

HINT
For Huevos Rancheros, place a warmed corn tortilla on a plate. Top with scrambled or poached eggs and *Salsa*. Garnish with sour cream, if desired.

SANDWICHES

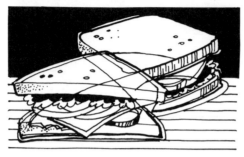

Sandwiches can be tempting fare. Let us introduce you to a few that will make old standbys pale by comparison. Add soup or a salad — and you have a meal.

POCKET BREAD SANDWICH

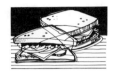

Add a cup of soup and you've got supper!

	FOR 1	FOR 2
pita or pocket bread	1	2
thinly sliced cooked roast beef, chicken or lamb	½ cup	1 cup
shredded lettuce or sprouts	½ cup	1 cup
chopped onion	2 tbs.	¼ cup
tomato, chopped	1 small	1 large
plain yogurt or sour cream	2 tbs.	¼ cup
chopped avocado or *Guacamole*, page 12	¼-½ cup	½-1 cup

Cut pita bread in half to make 2 pockets. If desired, wrap pita in foil and warm in a 300° oven for 10 to 15 minutes. Stir together meat, lettuce, onion, tomato and yogurt. Spoon filling into pocket bread and top with avocado or *Guacamole.*

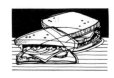

TACOS

Complete this meal with refried beans and fresh fruit.

	FOR 1	FOR 2
tortilla	1	2
oil	1½ tsp.	1 tbs.
ground beef or cooked shredded chicken	¼ lb.	½ lb.
chopped onion	1½ tsp.	1 tbs.
chili powder	dash	dash
shredded lettuce	¼ cup	½ cup
grated Monterey Jack or cheddar cheese	2 tbs.	¼ cup
chopped tomato	¼ cup	½ cup
chopped avocado or *Guacamole*, page 12	¼-½ cup	½-1 cup
sour cream	1 tbs.	2 tbs.
Salsa, page 31		

Heat oil in a skillet over high heat. Add tortillas, one at a time. Fry 30 seconds on each side. Drain well on paper towels, fold in half, and place in a warm oven until needed. In remaining oil, brown beef or chicken with onion and chili powder. Drain excess oil. Stuff tortillas with beef or chicken and top with remaining ingredients.

HINT

Just about any kind of leftover meat, including beef, lamb or pork, can be used to stuff tacos.

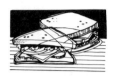

STUFFED TUNA ROLLS

These rolls make a perfect picnic carry-along, because they are great served cold.

	FOR 1	FOR 2
1 can (6½ oz.) tuna	½ can	1 can
grated cheddar cheese	¼ cup	½ cup
minced onion	1½ tsp.	1 tbs.
chili sauce	1 tbs.	2 tbs.
relish	1 tbs.	2 tbs.
mayonnaise	1 tbs.	2 tbs.
lemon juice	1½ tsp.	1 tbs.
French roll	1 large	2 large

Combine all ingredients except roll in a mixing bowl. Stir until blended. Slice about 1 inch off end of French roll. Scoop out center of roll and discard. Spoon tuna mixture into roll. Wrap roll in foil and bake for 30 minutes in a 350° oven. Repeat for 2. Serve hot or cold.

BAGEL WITH TOPPINGS

You can probably think up even more toppings for the versatile bagel.

	FOR 1	FOR 2
bagel, split and toasted	1	2
cream cheese, softened	1 oz.	2 oz.
one or more *Variations*, below		

Spread bagel with cream cheese and top with any of the following variations, or a combination.

VARIATIONS

- smoked salmon
- capers
- chopped hard-cooked egg
- sliced olives
- sliced cucumber
- shredded carrot

- watercress or sprouts
- chopped nuts
- raisins
- chopped dates
- jam or honey
- sliced avocados

- sliced tomatoes
- poppy seeds
- sesame seeds
- baby shrimp
- chopped pickle
- chutney

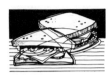

SLOPPY JOES

Serve this hot and hearty sandwich for a quick and easy meal. It goes nicely with **Coleslaw**, *page 52.*

	FOR 1	FOR 2
ground beef	¼ lb.	½ lb.
chopped onion	1½ tsp.	1 tbs.
chopped green bell pepper	1½ tsp.	1 tbs.
Barbecue Sauce, page 29	¼ cup	½ cup
cheddar or American cheese	1 slice	2 slices
bun	1	2

In a small skillet, brown beef over medium-high heat; drain fat. Add onion, pepper and *Barbecue Sauce*. Cover and simmer 15 minutes. Spoon meat over half of bun, top with cheese and broil until cheese melts. Top with other half of bun.

HOT SEAFOOD ENGLISH MUFFIN

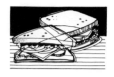

Any cooked fish may be stirred into this savory spread.

	FOR 1	FOR 2
grated Swiss cheese	¼ cup	½ cup
sliced mushrooms	¼ cup	½ cup
chopped green onions, or parsley	1 tsp.	1 tbs.
cooked shrimp, crab or tuna	¼ cup	½ cup
mayonnaise	2 tbs.	¼ cup
English muffin, split	1	2

Combine all ingredients except muffins in a mixing bowl. Stir until blended. Spread over muffins. Bake 10 minutes in a 400° oven. Then broil until bubbly.

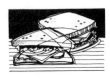

GRILLED SANDWICHES

Choose any of the fillings below for your sandwich. The egg-dipped bread will seal in the flavors of the filling, and will provide the bread with a crusty, golden exterior.

	FOR 1	FOR 2
bread	2 slices	4 slices
choice of filling, follows		
egg	1	2
milk	1 tbs.	2 tbs.
butter	1 tsp.	2 tsp.

Place filling on bread and top with second slice of bread. Beat egg with milk. Turn sandwich in mixture to coat both sides. Melt butter in a skillet over medium heat. Brown sandwich, pressing down with spatula after turning.

FILLINGS

- **Monte Cristo:** 1 slice of Swiss cheese and one or more slices of ham, chicken or turkey. Or try a combination of meats.

- **Rueben:** 1 slice of Swiss cheese, several slices of corned beef, 2 tbs. or more of sauerkraut and 1 tbs. or more of *Thousand Island Dressing*, page 66, on rye bread. Place on bread in order listed. Top with remaining slice of rye.

- **Italian:** 1 or more slices of mozzarella cheese with slices of salami.

- **Herb Garden:** 1 slice cheddar cheese, and 2 or 3 slices of tomato sprinkled with dill.

PIZZA

Makes: one 12-inch pizza

Some people prefer only a light sprinkling of cheese. Others feel cheated without everything traditionally used for topping. Either way, you'll enjoy this recipe.

½ pkg. active dry yeast
½ cup warm water (about 110°)
1¼ cups flour
½ tsp. sugar
¼ tsp. salt

1 tbs. oil
Pizza Sauce, follows
8 oz. mozzarella cheese, grated
Additions, follow

In a mixing bowl, combine yeast with warm water. Stir until dissolved. Add flour, sugar, salt and oil. Mix well. Knead dough until smooth and elastic, adding more flour if dough is sticky. Place in a greased bowl, turning to coat top. Cover with plastic wrap and a towel and place in a draft-free area. Let rise 1 hour. Punch dough down and roll out to form a 12-inch circle. Place on a greased baking sheet and pinch edges to form a slight rim. Bake in a 425° oven for 5 minutes. Spread pizza sauce over crust; top with cheese and additions. Bake 15 minutes, or until cheese is bubbly and crust is golden.

PIZZA SAUCE

½ cup *Tomato Sauce*, page 30
½ clove garlic, crushed
¼ tsp. oregano
¼ tsp. basil

Combine all ingredients in a saucepan and simmer for 5 minutes.

ADDITIONS

- sliced fresh mushrooms
- sausage or ground beef, cooked and crumbled
- sliced pepperoni
- sliced green, yellow or red bell pepper
- sliced tomato
- sliced or chopped onion
- sliced olives
- anchovies
- pesto
- Canadian bacon and pineapple
- feta cheese

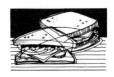

CLUB SANDWICH

A favorite when eating out, this can now be served at home.

	FOR 1	FOR 2
bread	3 slices	6 slices
butter or mayonnaise	2-3 tbs.	4-6 tbs.
lettuce leaves	2	4
tomato slices	4-6	8-12
pineapple slices, optional	2	4
chicken, turkey or ham	2-4 slices	4-8 slices

Toast bread, if desired. Spread one side of each slice with butter. Arrange lettuce leaves, tomato slices, pineapple slices and chicken slices on buttered side of two slices of bread. Stack bread, one on top of the other, ending with a plain slice. Cut in half diagonally twice, creating an X cut.

SALADS

Salads make an appearance, in one form or another, at almost every lunch and dinner. Some would consider a meal incomplete without a salad — and some are hearty enough to make an entire meal.

Salads are a boon to busy people. Simply by keeping a few ingredients on hand, you have the makings for a salad. Use the *Salad Chart* to create your own.

Salad Chart

Select one or more for your salad. Toss with dressing of choice.

GREENS	VEGETABLES	PROTEIN	GARNISHES
iceberg lettuce	carrots	beef	green onion
romaine lettuce	tomatoes	chicken	red onion
red leaf lettuce	celery	ham	bacon, cooked and
butter lettuce	green, yellow or red	salami	crumbled
spinach	bell pepper	seafood	imitation bacon bits
cabbage	avocado	cheese	sun-dried tomatoes
endive	cauliflower	hard-cooked eggs	croutons
watercress	radishes	nuts and seeds	olives
	cucumber	garbanzo beans	capers
	mushrooms	kidney beans	herbs
	zucchini		beets
	broccoli		alfalfa or bean
	asparagus		sprouts
	green beans		red cabbage
	artichoke hearts		water chestnuts
	corn		cooked bulghur
	peas		jicama

BEAN SALAD

Makes: 3 cups

Delicious on its own. We also add it to tossed green salads and sandwiches. **Blue Cheese Dressing**, *page 63, contrasts exceptionally well with Bean Salad served with lettuce.*

1 can (8 oz.) kidney beans
1 can (8 oz.) garbanzo beans
1 jar (6 oz.) marinated artichoke hearts, undrained
1 small onion, sliced
3 tbs. wine vinegar
1 tbs. sugar
¼ tsp. salt
½ tsp. celery seed
½ tsp. mustard seed

Rinse beans with water and drain. In a mixing bowl, combine all ingredients. Chill several hours or overnight before serving.

TOSTADA SALAD

You can also layer this salad on a tostada shell.

	FOR 1	FOR 2
shredded lettuce	1 cup	2 cups
refried beans	1 cup	2 cups
chili powder	1/8 tsp.	1/4 tsp.
cumin	1/8 tsp.	1/4 tsp.
garlic powder	1/8 tsp.	1/4 tsp.
ripe avocado, mashed	1	2
sour cream	1 tbs.	2 tbs.
sliced ripe olives	2 tbs.	1/4 cup
green onions, sliced	2	4
shredded cheddar cheese	1/2 cup	1 cup
tomato, chopped	1 small	1 medium
tortilla chips		

Arrange lettuce on a plate. Mix beans with seasonings and spread over lettuce. Combine avocado with sour cream and spread over beans. Layer remaining ingredients over avocado. Serve with tortilla chips.

SPINACH SALAD

*Serve this salad as an accompaniment to an entrée or as the main dish. Choose either the **Sweet and Sour** or **Soy Sesame Dressing** to top it.*

	FOR 1	FOR 2
fresh spinach	½ bunch	1 small bunch
bean sprouts	¼ cup	½ cup
sliced mushrooms	¼ cup	½ cup
hard-cooked egg, chopped	1	2
bacon, cooked and crumbled	1 slice or 1 tbs.	2 slices or 2 tbs.
green onion, sliced	½	1

Wash and dry spinach. Tear into bite-sized pieces in a salad bowl. Add remaining ingredients. Combine ingredients for dressing and mix well. (Dressing may be made ahead of time.) Toss salad with dressing and serve immediately.

SWEET AND SOUR DRESSING

2 tbs. oil
½ tsp. sugar
1 tbs. ketchup
1 tbs. wine vinegar
½ tsp. Worcestershire sauce
salt and pepper

SOY SESAME DRESSING

2 tbs. oil
1 tbs. lemon juice
1 tsp. soy sauce
1 tbs. toasted sesame seed
1 tsp. honey
½ clove garlic, crushed
dash cayenne pepper, optional
salt and pepper

COLESLAW

A food processor will make quick work of the cabbage and carrots. Great with barbecued meats or poultry.

	FOR 1	FOR 2
shredded cabbage	⅔ cup	1⅓ cups
shredded carrot or chopped apple	2 tbs.	¼ cup
raisins, optional	1 tbs.	2 tbs.
Dijon mustard	¼ tsp.	½ tsp.
vinegar or lemon juice	½ tsp.	1 tsp.
mayonnaise or sour cream	2 tbs.	¼ cup
celery seed	⅛ tsp.	¼ tsp.
salt and pepper		

Combine all ingredients in a mixing bowl. Toss together to mix thoroughly.

POTATO SALAD

Servings: 2

New potatoes are better for salads because they will not break apart when you toss them. Potato Salad can easily be made into a complete meal by adding ½ cup or more of diced, cooked ham or sausage.

2 cups cooked potatoes (3 medium),
  sliced or cubed
1 tsp. minced onion
⅓ cup mayonnaise

1 hard-cooked egg, chopped, optional
1 tsp. vinegar
salt and coarsely ground pepper

Add one of the following combinations:

#1
- 2 tbs. sliced celery
- 2 tbs. chopped sweet pickles
- ½ tsp. celery seed

#2
- ½ clove garlic, crushed
- 2 tbs. chopped green pepper
- 1 tbs. chopped parsley

Combine all ingredients in a mixing bowl. Toss gently until blended. Serve warm or chilled. For 1 serving, refrigerate remaining salad for another meal.

ROQUEFORT AND FRUIT SALAD

The distinct flavor of the cheese enhances the flavors of the apples and grapes. Serve on a lettuce leaf.

	FOR 1	FOR 2
apple, coarsely chopped	1	2
grapes	½ cup	1 cup
broken walnuts	2 tbs.	¼ cup
Roquefort or blue cheese, crumbled	1 tbs.	2 tbs.
sour cream	2 tbs.	¼ cup

In a mixing bowl, toss apples, grapes and walnuts together. Add remaining ingredients. Mix gently until combined.

CRAB LOUIS

Substitute fresh or canned shrimp for a shrimp Louis.

	FOR 1	FOR 2
lettuce leaves		
shredded lettuce	1 cup	2 cups
cooked crabmeat, or shrimp	½ cup	1 cup
hard-cooked egg, quartered	1	2
small tomato, quartered	1	2
cooked asparagus spears, optional	4	8
avocado, sliced, optional	1 small	1 large
lemon wedges		
Thousand Island Dressing, page 66		

Arrange lettuce leaves on plates. Top with shredded lettuce and crab. Garnish with remaining ingredients. Spoon *Thousand Island Dressing* over all.

CHICKEN AND FRUIT SALAD

You can substitute ham for chicken in this refreshing salad.

	FOR 1	FOR 2
pineapple or melon	½	1
seedless grapes	½ cup	1 cup
banana, sliced	½	1
flaked coconut	2 tbs.	¼ cup
sliced almonds	2 tbs.	¼ cup
chopped dates, optional	3 tbs.	⅓ cup
cubed cooked chicken or ham	½ cup	1 cup
lemon or orange yogurt	2 tbs.	¼ cup
ground ginger	⅛ tsp.	¼ tsp.

Cut pineapple in half. Remove fruit leaving ½-inch shell. Cut fruit in chunks. If using melon, cut in half zig-zag fashion. Remove and discard seed. Scoop out fruit using a melon baller. Combine either pineapple chunks or melon balls with remaining filling ingredients. Stir well. Spoon filling into fruit shells.

CAESAR SALAD

Here is our version of a popular classic.

	FOR 1	FOR 2
garlic clove	1	1
romaine lettuce	½ small head	1 small head
oil	1 tbs.	2 tbs.
salt and pepper		
egg yolk	1	1
lemon juice	1½ tsp.	1 tbs.
croutons	1 tbs.	2 tbs.
grated Parmesan cheese	1 tbs.	2 tbs.
anchovy, optional	½	1

Rub a salad bowl with cut garlic clove. Into bowl, tear lettuce into bite-sized pieces. Add oil, salt and pepper and toss to coat lettuce leaves. Add egg yolk and lemon juice and toss thoroughly. Toss again with croutons and cheese.

STUFFED TOMATOES

Egg- or rice salad-filled tomatoes make a pretty presentation.

	FOR 1	**FOR 2**
large tomato	1	2

Slice tops off tomatoes. Scoop out centers carefully, leaving a ½-inch wall. Sprinkle with salt, turn upside down and drain for 20 minutes. Fill with salad.

CURRIED EGG SALAD

	FOR 1	FOR 2
mayonnaise	1½ tbs.	3 tbs.
hard-cooked egg, chopped	1	2
sliced green onion	½	1
curry powder	dash	dash
soy sauce	¼ tsp.	½ tsp.
lemon juice	½ tsp.	1 tsp.
chopped parsley	1½ tsp.	1 tbs.

Combine all ingredients except parsley in a mixing bowl. Toss gently to blend. Fill tomatoes and garnish with parsley, if desired.

RICE SALAD

	FOR 1	FOR 2
cooked rice	⅓ cup	⅔ cup
mayonnaise or sour cream	1 tbs.	2 tbs.
capers	1 tsp.	2 tsp.
cooked shrimp, optional	¼ cup	½ cup
salt and pepper		
chopped parsley, optional	1½ tsp.	1 tbs.

Combine all ingredients except parsley in a mixing bowl. Toss gently to blend. Fill tomatoes and garnish with parsley, if desired.

NICOISE SALAD

This classic salad combines vegetables with wonderful Mediterranean flavors.

	FOR 1	FOR 2
olive oil	2 tbs.	1/3 cup
lemon juice or wine vinegar	1 tbs.	2 tbs.
Dijon mustard	1/2 tsp.	1 tsp.
garlic clove, minced	1/2	1
salt and pepper		
new potato, cooked and sliced	1	2
green beans, cooked tender-crisp	1/2 cup	1 cup
tomato, quartered	1	2
green onion, sliced	1	2
lettuce leaves		
6-7 oz. can tuna, drained	1/2 can	1 can
capers	1 tbs.	2 tbs.
Niçoise olives	2 tbs.	1/4 cup
minced fresh parsley	1 tbs.	2 tbs.

Combine olive oil, lemon juice, mustard, garlic, salt and pepper in a small bowl. Set aside until ready to use. Arrange lettuce leaves on 1 or 2 plates. Arrange potatoes, green beans, tomatoes and green onion attractively on lettuce. Flake tuna in center of salad and top with capers, olives and parsley. Spoon dressing over salad and serve.

VERMICELLI SALAD

Add shrimp for a refreshing luncheon entrée.

	FOR 1	FOR 2
vermicelli, uncooked	2 oz.	4 oz.
olive oil	½ tbs.	1 tbs.
red wine vinegar	1 tbs.	2 tbs.
garlic clove	½	1
6 oz. jar marinated artichokes,	½ jar	1 jar
sliced mushrooms	¼ cup	½ cup
cherry tomatoes, halved	5	10
toasted chopped walnuts	2 tbs.	¼ cup
chopped fresh parsley	1 tbs.	2 tbs.
cooked shrimp, optional	¼ cup	½ cup
salt and pepper		

Cook pasta as directed on page 84. Combine oil, vinegar and garlic in a small bowl. Mix with pasta and chill. Drain and chop artichokes, add remaining ingredients and toss with chilled pasta just before serving.

VINAIGRETTE DRESSING

Makes: ½ cup

Vegetables such as broccoli, green beans, asparagus or Brussels sprouts, cooked until just tender, are delicious dressed with this.

6 tbs. olive oil
2 tbs. wine vinegar or lemon juice

salt and pepper

Combine oil, vinegar, salt and pepper with any of the following variations. Mix thoroughly.

VARIATIONS

- ½ clove garlic, crushed
- 1 tsp. chopped chives or parsley
- ⅛ tsp. dry mustard or ½ tsp. Dijon mustard
- ¼ tsp. tarragon, dill or basil
- 1 tbs. grated Parmesan cheese
- 1 tsp. capers

BLUE CHEESE DRESSING

Makes: ½ cup

You'll like this flavorful dressing spooned over crisp salad greens.

2 tbs. crumbled blue cheese or
   Roquefort
⅓ cup mayonnaise or sour cream

2 tbs. milk
dash garlic powder, optional
salt and pepper

Combine all ingredients in a small bowl. Stir to blend. Chill.

YOGURT DRESSING

Makes: ⅓ cup

Toss with thinly sliced cucumbers or zucchini.

⅓ cup plain yogurt
1 tsp. chopped chives or green onion

dash dill
salt and pepper

Combine all ingredients in a small bowl. Stir until blended. Chill.

FRUIT DRESSINGS

Dress up a fresh fruit compote or any fruit salad with one of these flavorful additions.

POPPY SEED DRESSING
Makes: 1/4 cup

2 tbs. oil
1 tbs. lemon juice
1 tbs. honey

1/2 tsp. poppy seeds
1/8 tsp. dry mustard

Combine all ingredients in a mixing bowl. Stir to blend and chill.

SOUR CREAM DRESSING
Makes: 1/3 cup

1/4 cup sour cream
1 tbs. honey

1 tbs. orange juice
dash ground ginger

Combine all ingredients in a small bowl. Stir to blend and chill.

MAYONNAISE VARIATIONS

Mayonnaise is a versatile dressing. Many sauces, dips and salad dressings use it as their base. Here are a few of the more popular.

THOUSAND ISLAND DRESSING
Makes: 1/3 cup

Serve this with shrimp or crab Louis.

1/4 cup mayonnaise
1 tbs. milk

1 tbs. chili sauce
freshly ground pepper

Combine all ingredients in a small bowl. Stir to blend and chill.

AIOLI OR GARLIC MAYONNAISE
Makes: 1/4 cup

Makes an excellent dip for artichokes, crab and shrimp. Let a dollop of it melt on top of fresh steamed vegetables, such as asparagus or new potatoes.

1/4 cup mayonnaise
1/4 tsp. Dijon mustard

1/2 clove garlic, crushed

Combine all ingredients in a small bowl. Stir to blend and chill.

TARTAR SAUCE

Any kind of fish or shellfish may be dipped into this classic sauce.

1/4 cup mayonnaise
2 tbs. finely chopped pickle
2 tsp. finely chopped green onion or parsley
1 tsp. lemon juice

Combine all ingredients in a mixing bowl. Stir to blend and chill.

EGGS AND CHEESE

Pound for pound, eggs are one of the least expensive forms of protein available. Additionally, almost every dish made with eggs is simple to prepare. The variety of egg dishes is almost limitless. Eggs and cheese are combined to form the base for a variety of our recipes from light, golden *Cheese Soufflé* to spicy *Cheese Enchiladas*. Omelets and quiches are wonderful for using odds and ends of leftover meats and vegetables. For entertaining, *Cheese Fondue* and *Eggs Benedict* are ideal.

OMELET

If you need to limit egg intake, you can also make a tasty omelet with one of the egg substitutes found in your grocer's dairy case.

	FOR 1	FOR 2
butter	2 tsp.	1½ tbs.
eggs	2	4
milk or water	1 tbs.	2 tbs.
parsley, tarragon or dill	⅛ tsp.	¼ tsp.
salt and pepper		
Filling Variations, follow		

Prepare 1 or more filling variations and set aside. In a small bowl, beat eggs with milk, parsley, salt and pepper. Heat butter in an 9-inch omelet pan or skillet over high heat until butter sizzles. Be careful not to let butter burn. Pour egg mixture into pan. (If making 2 omelets, pour only ½ egg mixture into pan. Prepare second omelet after first is completed.) Tilt pan to spread mixture around edges. Loosen edges of omelet as it cooks to distribute uncooked portion underneath. When top of omelet is set to a soft custard, spoon filing over middle third of omelet. Lift each third of unfilled sides of omelet over filling. Slide out of pan onto a warm plate to serve.

FILLING VARIATIONS

	FOR 1	FOR 2
grated cheese, such as cheddar, Monterey Jack or Swiss	2 tbs.	1/4 cup
diced cooked vegetables, such as asparagus, zucchini, tomatoes, potatoes, broccoli or squash	2 tbs.	1/4 cup
bacon, cooked and crumbled	1 tbs.	2 tbs.
chopped chives or green onions	1 tbs.	2 tbs.
sautéed sliced mushrooms	1/4 cup	1/2 cup

CHILI RELLENOS CASSEROLE

This south-of-the-border egg dish is perfect for a brunch.

	FOR 1	FOR 2
can (4 oz.) whole green chiles	½ can	1 can
grated Monterey Jack cheese	¼ cup	½ cup
grated cheddar cheese	¼ cup	½ cup
egg	1	2
sour cream	¼ cup	½ cup
milk	⅓ cup	⅔ cup
salt	⅛ tsp.	¼ tsp.
flour	1½ tbs.	3 tbs.
baking powder	dash	⅛ tsp.
Salsa, page 31, optional		

Slit chiles lengthwise and remove seeds. Arrange in a buttered baking dish. Sprinkle cheese over chiles. Mix remaining ingredients together and pour over chiles. Bake in a 350° oven for 40 minutes, or until set. Top with *Salsa* if desired.

CHEESE STRATA

A light and delectable dish, this may be varied by using different cheeses.

	FOR 1	FOR 2
French bread, crusts removed	1 slice	2 slices
butter	1 tsp.	2 tsp.
grated cheddar cheese	⅓ cup	⅔ cup
egg	1	2
dry white wine	2 tbs.	¼ cup
Tabasco Sauce or nutmeg	dash	dash
Tomato Sauce, page 30, optional	2 tbs.	¼ cup

Spread butter over bread and place in a buttered ramekin. Sprinkle cheese over bread. In a small bowl, beat together egg, wine and Tabasco sauce. Pour mixture over cheese. Bake in a 350° oven for 30 minutes. Top with *Tomato Sauce* if desired.

CHEESE SOUFFLÉ

This is an elegant way to use leftover meats and vegetables.

	FOR 1	FOR 2
butter	1½ tsp.	1 tbs.
flour	1½ tsp.	1 tbs.
milk or light cream	3 tbs.	⅓ cup
grated cheddar cheese	⅓ cup	⅔ cup
egg yolk	1	2
nutmeg, cayenne pepper or dry mustard	dash	dash
salt and pepper		
egg white	1	2

Melt butter in a saucepan over medium heat. Stir in flour and let bubble for 30 seconds. Add milk and cook, stirring until thick. Add cheese and stir until melted. Remove from heat. Mix in egg yolks, seasonings and one or more variations. Beat egg whites until they form moist peaks. Fold egg whites into yolk mixture. Spoon into one or two 10-oz. soufflé dishes and bake 20 minutes in a 350° oven. Serve immediately.

VARIATIONS

	FOR 1	FOR 2
minced chives or green onions	1 tbs.	2 tbs.
chopped cooked vegetable	2 tbs.	¼ cup
chopped cooked meat, poultry or seafood	2 tbs.	¼ cup

QUICHE

You can make endless variations with this basic quiche.

	FOR 1	FOR 2
single crust pastry, page 164	half recipe	whole recipe
beaten egg	1	2
light cream, milk or plain yogurt	¼ cup	½ cup
grated cheese such as Swiss or cheddar	¼ cup	½ cup
chopped meat, poultry, seafood or vegetable	¼ cup	½ cup
dill, basil or tarragon	dash	¼ tsp.
salt		

Line one or two 4½-inch tart pans with pastry. Prick pastry shells all over with a fork and bake for 5 minutes in a 425° oven. Beat remaining ingredients together in a mixing bowl. Pour into prebaked pastry shells. Bake in a 350° oven for 30 minutes, or until knife inserted into center comes out clean.

QUICHE WITH NUTS

Nuts provide a nice contrast to the creamy texture of quiche. Substitute any one of these combinations for the ½ cup cooked chopped meat called for in the preceding recipe.

- 2 tbs. sliced almonds with ½ cup cooked, chopped chicken
- 2 tbs. chopped cashews with ½ cup cooked, sliced zucchini
- 2 tbs. chopped walnuts with ½ cup cooked, sliced broccoli

QUICHE LORRAINE

Substitute these ingredients for cheese, meat and herb in the basic quiche recipe.

- ½ cup grated Swiss cheese
- 2 slices bacon cooked and crumbled
- dash nutmeg

CHEESE ENCHILADA

*Serve with refried beans or **Rice Verde**, page 92.*

	FOR 1	FOR 2
oil	1 tbs.	2 tbs.
tortillas	2	4
chopped onion	2 tbs.	1/4 cup
clove garlic, crushed	1/2	1
Tomato Sauce, page 30	1/2 cup	1 cup
cumin	1/8 tsp.	1/4 tsp.
chili powder	1/8 tsp.	1/4 tsp.
salt and pepper		
grated cheddar cheese	1 cup	2 cups
hard-cooked egg, chopped	1	2
green onion, sliced	1	2
sliced ripe olives	1/4 cup	1/2 cup

Heat oil in a pan over medium-high heat. Fry tortillas lightly on both sides. Place on paper towels to drain. Reduce heat to medium-low. Sauté onion and garlic in remaining oil until tender. Add *Tomato Sauce* and seasonings. Stir until mixture is heated through. Dip tortillas in sauce. Combine half of cheese, egg, onion and olives in a mixing bowl. Divide mixture among tortillas and fill. Roll tortillas to enclose filling and place in a lightly greased baking dish. Top with remaining sauce and cheese. Bake in a 350° oven for 15 minutes, or until hot and bubbly.

CHEESE FONDUE

The word fondue is derived from the French word "fondre," which means to melt. The Swiss claim credit for the origin of fondue.

	FOR 1	FOR 2
Swiss cheese, grated	2 oz.	4 oz.
Gruyère cheese, grated	2½ oz.	5 oz.
flour	1 tbs.	2 tbs.
white wine	½ cup	1 cup
sherry	1 tbs.	2 tbs.
nutmeg	dash	dash
French bread cubes		
ham cubes and/or apple cubes, optional		

Shake cheese with flour in a plastic bag. Let stand at room temperature for at least 2 hours. Heat wine in a saucepan until bubbles start to rise. Add cheese and stir until blended. Stir in sherry and nutmeg. Pour cheese mixture into a fondue pot and keep warm. Serve with bread, ham and apple cubes for dipping.

EGGS BENEDICT

Serve this elegant dish to guests for breakfast or brunch and get rave reviews!

	FOR 1	FOR 2
English muffin, split and toasted	1	2
butter		
Canadian bacon or ham, sautéed	2 slices	4 slices
vinegar	1 tsp.	2 tsp.
eggs	2	4
Hollandaise Sauce, page 26	⅓ cup	⅔ cup

Spread toasted English muffins with butter. Top each muffin half with 1 slice of Canadian bacon. Place in a 200° oven and keep warm. Place water to a depth of 1 inch in a saucepan. Add vinegar and bring to a boil. Reduce heat to simmer. Gently break eggs into water and cook 3 to 5 minutes, or to desired degree of doneness. Remove eggs with a slotted spoon. Place 1 egg on each muffin half and pour *Hollandaise Sauce* over eggs. Serve immediately.

PASTA, RICE AND BREAD

Pasta, rice and bread can be called the "diplomats" of any meal. Each blends harmoniously with almost any dish. Proper cooking methods are essential to their success. Our easy-to-follow recipes eliminate the guess work and make perfect results possible every time.

Enjoy *Pasta Primavera* any time of year with the abundance of fresh vegetables available. When cooking rice to go along with a main dish such as *Stir-Fried Beef and Vegetables*, cook enough extra to make *Rice Verde* and serve with tacos later in the week.

Hot biscuits or freshly baked muffins can turn an otherwise plain meal into something special with a minimum of effort.

PERFECT PASTA

Perfect pasta can be yours, if you follow these directions. Oil added to the water prevents the pasta from sticking together and keeps the water from boiling over.

	FOR 1	**FOR 2**
water	1 quart	2 quarts
salt	¼ tsp.	½ tsp.
oil	2 tsp.	1 tbs.
uncooked pasta	2 oz.	4 oz.
butter or olive oil, optional	1 tbs.	2 tbs.
grated Parmesan cheese, optional		

Bring water, salt and oil to a rolling boil in a saucepan about twice the size a the amount of water called for. Add pasta and boil uncovered until tender, but pasta still offers a slight resistance to teeth when bitten (*al dente*) The cooking time will vary according to the type of pasta. Drain cooked pasta in a colander. Shake the colander until pasta is well drained, and do not rinse it. Toss with butter and grated cheese or *Pesto*, page 85, or top with a piping hot sauce. Serve immediately.

PASTA WITH FRESH PESTO

Pesto is a nice change from the more familiar pasta sauces. Fresh basil is one of summer's greatest delights. Enjoy fresh pesto often during the season and make extra for the freezer.

	FOR 1	FOR 2
uncooked pasta: spaghetti, linguini, noodles	2 oz.	4 oz.
fresh basil leaves	½ cup	1 cup
clove garlic, crushed	1	2
pine nuts	1½ tsp.	1 tbs.
olive oil	2 tbs.	¼ cup
freshly grated Parmesan cheese	1 tbs.	2 tbs.

Cook pasta as directed on page 84. While pasta is cooking, place remaining ingredients in a blender or food processor and blend until smooth. Toss pesto with hot, well drained pasta.

PASTA PRIMAVERA

Select several vegetables in season for a colorful pasta dish.

	FOR 1	FOR 2
uncooked pasta	2 oz.	4 oz.
oil	1 tbs.	2 tbs.
vegetables, coarsely chopped: broccoli, green beans, zucchini, yellow squash, green and red bell peppers	1 cup	2 cups
sliced mushrooms	½ cup	1 cup
tomato, chopped	½	1
garlic clove, minced	½	1
salt and pepper		
grated Parmesan cheese		

Cook pasta as directed on page 84. While pasta cooks, heat olive oil in a skillet. Add vegetables and sauté, stirring occasionally, for 5 minutes. Add mushrooms, tomatoes and garlic; sauté 5 minutes, or until vegetables are just tender. Toss vegetables with hot pasta, season with salt and pepper, and sprinkle with Parmesan.

PASTA PROVENÇAL

This piquant pasta sauce is flavored with tomatoes, olives and capers.

	FOR 1	FOR 2
uncooked pasta	2 oz.	4 oz.
olive oil	1 tbs.	2 tbs.
chopped tomatoes	1 cup	2 cups
garlic clove, minced	1	2
chopped Niçoise olives	2 tbs.	¼ cup
capers	1 tbs.	2 tbs.
salt and pepper		

Cook pasta as directed on page 84. While pasta cooks, heat olive oil in a saucepan. Add tomatoes, garlic, olives and capers. Simmer for 10 to 15 minutes. Toss pasta with sauce and season with salt and pepper. Serve hot.

SEAFOOD PASTA

This is an elegant and easily prepared dish.

	FOR 1	FOR 2
uncooked pasta	2 oz.	4 oz.
butter	½ tbs.	1 tbs.
sliced mushrooms	½ cup	1 cup
peas	¼ cup	½ cup
cooked crab or shrimp	¼ cup	½ cup
light cream	3 tbs.	⅓ cup
salt and pepper		
grated Parmesan cheese	2 tbs.	¼ cup

Cook pasta as directed on page 84. Sauté mushrooms in butter until tender. Add peas, crab or shrimp and light cream and cook until heated through. Toss pasta with sauce and Parmesan cheese and serve.

BAKED NOODLES RICOTTA

*You'll find this a delicious side dish to serve with **Veal Piccata** on page 115.*

	FOR 1	FOR 2
cooked noodles	½ cup	1 cup
melted butter	1½ tsp.	1 tbs.
ricotta	¼ cup	½ cup
egg, beaten	½	1
garlic powder, optional	dash	dash
salt and pepper		
grated Parmesan cheese	2 tbs.	¼ cup

Combine all ingredients in a mixing bowl. Stir until blended. Place in 1 or 2 buttered ramekins. If desired, sprinkle with additional Parmesan cheese. Bake in a 350° oven for 20 minutes, or until hot and bubbly.

RICE AND VARIATIONS

Replace the water with beef, chicken or vegetable broth for extra flavor.

	FOR 1	FOR 2
water	⅔ cup	1⅓ cups
butter	2 tsp.	1 tbs.
salt	dash	¼ tsp.
long grain white rice	⅓ cup	⅔ cup

Combine water, butter and salt in a saucepan. Bring to a boil. Reduce heat to low, add rice, cover and cook for 20 minutes, or until liquid is absorbed and rice is tender.

VARIATIONS

Add any of the following to cooked rice:

- 1-2 tbs. slivered almonds or pine nuts
- 2-4 tbs. grated cheese
- 1-2 tsp. minced green onion, parsley or chives
- ¼-½ cup sautéed mushrooms

ARMENIAN RICE

Wonderful with lamb or chicken.

	FOR 1	FOR 2
butter	1 tsp.	2 tsp.
vermicelli, broken	1/4 coil	1/2 coil
long grain rice	3 tbs.	1/3 cup
salt and pepper		
water	1/2 cup plus 2 tbs.	1 1/4 cups
pine nuts, sautéed until golden in 2 tsp. butter, optional	1 tbs.	2 tbs.

Melt butter in a skillet over medium heat. Add vermicelli and brown. Add rice, salt, pepper and water. Bring to a boil, reduce heat, cover and cook over low heat for about 25 minutes, or until liquid is absorbed. Remove from heat and set aside for 5 minutes. Add pine nuts if desired and serve.

RICE VERDE

This colorful rice dish is great served with Mexican food. Try it with our **Tacos** *on page 34.*

	FOR 1	FOR 2
cooked rice	⅔ cup	1⅓ cups
sour cream	2 tbs.	¼ cup
chopped green chiles or green onions	1 tbs.	2 tbs.
grated cheddar or Monterey Jack cheese	¼ cup	½ cup

Place half of the rice in a buttered ramekin. Combine sour cream, chiles and half the cheese in a mixing bowl. Spread over rice and cover with remaining rice. Top with cheese. Bake in a 350° oven for 15 minutes.

BULGHUR PILAFF

*A nutritious alternative to rice, this is ideal with **Shish Kabobs**, page 124.*

	FOR 1	FOR 2
butter	2 tsp.	4 tsp.
chopped onion	1 tbs.	2 tbs.
bulghur	¼ cup	½ cup
chicken stock	½ cup	1 cup
cinnamon	dash	dash
celery seed	dash	dash
pine nuts, optional	1 tbs.	2 tbs.

Melt butter in a saucepan over medium heat. Add onion and bulghur. Sauté until golden. Add remaining ingredients and bring to a boil. Reduce heat, cover and cook over low heat for 15 minutes, or until liquid is absorbed. Stir in pine nuts.

BISCUITS

Makes: 6

Piping hot biscuits are melt-in-your-mouth good.

1 cup flour
1½ tsp. baking power
1¼ tsp. salt
3 tbs. butter
⅓ cup milk

Stir flour, baking powder and salt together in a mixing bowl. Cut in butter until mixture resembles coarse cornmeal. Add milk and stir lightly. Knead gently 12 times. Roll or pat dough to ½-inch thickness. Cut into squares or rounds and place on an ungreased baking sheet. Bake in a 450° oven for 12 minutes, or until golden brown.

HOT CHEESE BREAD

Makes: ½ cup spread

Great with soup or salad!

1 tbs. butter, at room temperature
3 tbs. mayonnaise
2 tsp. sliced green onions or chopped chives
2 tsp. minced parsley
½ cup grated cheddar cheese
2 French rolls or 4 slices French bread

Combine butter, mayonnaise, onions, parsley and cheese in a mixing bowl. Stir until blended. Split rolls and spread with cheese mixture. Broil until bubbly.

MUFFINS

Makes: 6

These light and tender muffins are best served hot from the oven.

1 cup flour
1½ tsp. baking powder
¼ tsp. salt
2 tbs. sugar or honey

⅓ cup milk
1 egg
3 tbs. oil

Stir dry ingredients together and make a well in the center. Combine liquid ingredients and add to dry ingredients. Stir until just moistened. Let sit for 1 minute. Fill greased or paper-lined muffin cups ⅔ full. Bake in a 400° oven for 18 to 20 minutes or until golden brown.

VARIATIONS

Stir 1 or more of the following ingredients into the batter before baking:

- 1 tbs. cooked, crumbled bacon
- 1 tbs. thinly sliced green onion
- ¼ cup shredded cheese
- ¼ cup chopped dates or nuts

- ⅓ cup blueberries
- 1 tsp. grated orange or lemon peel
- ¼ cup raisins and ½ tsp. cinnamon
- ¼ cup grated carrot or apple

VEGETABLES

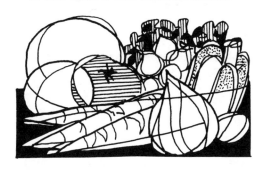

Plan your menus to take advantage of the abundance of fresh vegetables available throughout the year. Add these recipes to your vegetable favorites.

ARTICHOKES IN WHITE WINE

*Select firm artichokes with tightly closed leaves. For variety, chill, scoop out choke and stuff with **Rice Salad**, page 58. Excellent with any lamb dish.*

	FOR 1	FOR 2
artichoke	1	2
clove garlic, chopped	½	1
chopped parsley	1 tsp.	2 tsp.
salt and pepper		
olive oil	1 tbs.	2 tbs.
white wine	¼ cup	½ cup

Remove small outer leaves from bottom of artichokes. Cut off stems so artichokes can sit upright and cut off thorny tips of leaves with scissors. Place in a small saucepan. Combine garlic, parsley, salt, pepper and oil; spoon between artichoke leaves. Pour wine into pan, cover and simmer 45 to 60 minutes or until leaves pull off easily. Add water if necessary.

ASPARAGUS WITH MUSTARD SAUCE

Spoon mustard sauce over hot or chilled asparagus spears.

	FOR 1	FOR 2
asparagus spears	6-8	12-16
sour cream	2 tbs.	¼ cup
Dijon mustard	½ tsp.	1 tsp.

Snap tough ends off asparagus. Steam or boil in a small amount of water for 10 minutes, or until just tender. Combine sour cream with mustard and spoon over asparagus.

BAKED WINTER SQUASH

Winter squash is delicious when spiced with nutmeg and glazed with molasses and brown sugar. Bake this along with **Meat Loaf***, page 110.*

	FOR 1	FOR 2
acorn or other winter squash	½	1
butter	1 tbs.	2 tbs.
molasses	1 tsp.	2 tsp.
brown sugar	1 tsp.	2 tsp.
nutmeg	dash	dash
salt and pepper		

Cut squash in half and scoop out seeds. Arrange, cut-side down, in a shallow baking pan. Surround with a small amount of hot water and bake in a 350° oven 30 minutes. Combine butter, molasses, brown sugar and seasonings. Pour off liquid from baking pan and turn squash cut-side up. Spread glaze over squash. Bake 30 minutes, or until tender, basting now and then with sauce.

BROCCOLI WITH BROWNED BUTTER

Broccoli becomes irresistible with a hint of nutmeg.

	FOR 1	FOR 2
broccoli	1 stalk	2 stalks
butter	1 tbs.	2 tbs.
nutmeg	dash	dash
salt and pepper		

Cut broccoli into florets. Steam or boil in a small amount of water for 10 minutes, or until just tender. Melt butter with nutmeg over low heat until butter is light brown, not scorched. Pour butter over broccoli. Add salt and pepper as desired.

DILLED GREEN BEANS

Dill adds zest to tender green beans. This vegetable creation is good served with seafood.

	FOR 1	FOR 2
fresh green beans, cut into 1½-inch pieces	1 cup	2 cups
butter	2 tsp.	1 tbs.
dill	dash	dash
lemon juice	½ tsp.	1 tsp.
salt and pepper		

Boil green beans in a small amount of water for 10 minutes, or until just tender. Drain well. Add butter, dill, lemon juice, salt and pepper. Stir until beans are well coated with seasonings.

GARLIC POTATO STRIPS

Roasted until golden, these garlic-flavored potatoes go well with steaks, roast or chicken.

	FOR 1	FOR 2
potato	1	2
butter	1 tbs.	2 tbs.
garlic clove, crushed	½	1
salt		

Quarter potatoes lengthwise and peel if desired. Boil for 10 minutes and drain. Melt butter in a baking pan. Add garlic and potato strips, turning to coat with butter and garlic. Sprinkle with salt. Bake in a 350° oven for 45 minutes, turning once or twice.

GLAZED CARROTS

A hint of mustard accents these beautifully glazed carrots.

	FOR 1	FOR 2
butter	2 tsp.	4 tsp.
sliced carrots	3⁄4 cup	1½ cups
brown sugar	2 tsp.	4 tsp.
prepared mustard	¼ tsp.	½ tsp.
salt and pepper		

Melt butter in a heavy saucepan or small skillet with a lid. Stir in remaining ingredients. Cover and simmer for 25 minutes, or until carrots are tender.

HERBED TOMATO

This vegetable is a delicious and colorful garnish for the meat platter.

	FOR 1	FOR 2
tomato, halved	1	2
butter	1 tsp.	2 tsp.
basil	dash	dash
oregano	dash	dash
salt and pepper		
grated Parmesan cheese		

Place tomato halves in a baking pan. Dot each half with butter and sprinkle with herbs, salt, pepper and cheese. Bake in a 350° oven for 20 minutes, or broil for 3 minutes or until heated through and cheese is lightly browned. watch carefully.

SCALLOPED POTATOES

Add ham for an entrée. Serve with a crisp green salad and a hot vegetable.

	FOR 1	FOR 2
potato, peeled and sliced	1 medium	2 medium
flour	1 tbs.	2 tbs.
salt and pepper		
minced onion	1 tsp.	2 tsp.
grated cheese	¼ cup	½ cup
chopped cooked ham, optional	¼ cup	½ cup
milk	½ cup	1 cup
butter	1 tsp.	2 tsp.

Place half of potato slices in a small buttered baking dish. Sprinkle with flour, salt, pepper, onion, cheese and ham. Top with remaining potato slices. Pour milk over all and dot with butter. Bake uncovered in a 350° oven for 1 hour.

SUMMER SQUASH CASSEROLE

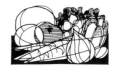

Squash, onion, green pepper and cheese provide a delectable combination of flavors.

	FOR 1	FOR 2
summer squash, cubed	1 cup	2 cups
chopped onion	1 tbs.	2 tbs.
chopped green bell pepper	1 tbs.	2 tbs.
grated cheddar cheese	¼ cup	½ cup
sour cream	2 tbs.	¼ cup
croutons	3 tbs.	6 tbs.

Cook squash, onion and pepper in a small amount of water until just tender. Drain vegetables well. Combine with cheese, sour cream and ⅔ of the croutons. Place in a buttered ramekin and top with remaining croutons. Bake in a 350° oven for 20 minutes or until hot and bubbly.

MEATS

A large portion of everyone's food budget goes for meat, but there are ways to economize. With our imaginative recipes, tailored to serve 1 or 2, you need not be limited to expensive steaks and chops. Combinations of flavors such as *Beef Carbonnade, Mock Ravioli* and *Veal Piccata* are much more exciting.

Many supermarket meat departments are beginning to package in smaller portions. If yours doesn't, put in a request to the manager. Don't buy more than you really want or need.

We believe you'll find our make-ahead ground beef mix one of your favorite timesavers. The convenience of having delicious hamburger patties, meatballs or meat loaf shaped and ready to cook at the end of a busy day more than makes up for the few minutes it takes to prepare it for the freezer. We have found the best time to mix and freeze the meat is just as soon as you bring it home from the market.

GROUND BEEF MAKE-AHEAD MIX FOR HAMBURGERS, MEATBALLS, MEAT LOAF

Make enough just for tonight, or for convenience, prepare our make-ahead mix for 8. Shape into patties, balls or loaves and freeze for future quick and easy meals.

	FOR 2	FOR 8
ground beef	½ lb.	2 lb.
egg	1	4
bread crumbs or wheat germ	2 tbs.	½ cup
milk	1 tbs.	¼ cup
chopped onion	2 tbs.	½ cup
salt	¼ tsp.	1 tsp.
pepper	⅛ tsp.	¼ tsp.

VARIATIONS

	FOR 2	FOR 8
Worcestershire sauce	½ tsp.	2 tsp.
chopped parsley	2 tbs.	½ cup
grated cheese	¼ cup	1 cup
chopped green bell pepper	1 tbs.	¼ cup

Mix all ingredients together, adding one or more variations if desired. Form into patties, balls or loaves. Make-Ahead Mix for 2 makes 2 meat patties or 12 meatballs, or 1 individual meat loaf. Make-Ahead Mix for 8 makes 8 hamburger patties, 48 meatballs or 1 large or 4 individual meat loaves. Freeze in serving-sized portions.

For hamburger patties: Fry 5 minutes on each side or broil 4 minutes on each side for medium doneness. Baste hamburgers with soy sauce or *Barbecue Sauce*, page 29, while cooking if desired. Serve in a bun with traditional garnishes or top with any of the following: sautéed mushrooms, cheese, sour cream mixed with chopped chives or bacon bits, or *Bearnaise Sauce*, page 27.

For meatballs: Bake in a 375° oven for 30 minutes or fry in 1 tbs. oil for 10 minutes, turning to brown. Add cooked meatballs to *Barbecue Sauce*, page 29, or *Sweet and Sour Sauce*, page 28, and heat through.

For meat loaf: Place mix for 8 in a large 9x5-inch baking pan. Bake in a 350° oven about 1½ hours. Place mix for 2 in one 6x3x2-inch loaf pan and bake in a 250° oven for 45 minutes. If desired, top with ¼ cup *Tomato Sauce*, page 30, before baking.

MEAT SAUCE FOR SPAGHETTI
Servings: 2

Hot Cheese Bread, page 95, and a tossed green salad complete this favorite meal. If time allows, make the sauce ahead — the flavor is even better when reheated.

½ lb. ground beef
¼ cup chopped onion
½ clove garlic, minced
½ cup sliced mushrooms
1 cup *Tomato Sauce*, page 30
dash oregano
dash basil
2 tbs. red wine, optional

Brown meat and onions in a frying pan over medium-high heat. Drain fat. Stir in remaining ingredients and simmer 30 minutes. Serve over hot cooked spaghetti. For 1 serving, refrigerate or freeze remaining half of sauce for another meal.

BEEF CARBONNADE

Servings: 2

Beer adds flavor to this robust stew. Serve over hot buttered noodles.

1 tbs. oil
½ lb. beef stew meat, cut into 1-inch
 cubes
1 small onion, sliced
½ clove garlic, chopped
1 tbs. flour

salt and pepper
½ cup beer or beef broth
1 tbs. brown sugar
½ bay leaf
dash thyme

Heat oil in a skillet. Brown meat, remove from skillet and set aside. Add onions and garlic to skillet. Cook, stirring, until limp. Return meat to pan, sprinkle with flour and season with salt and pepper. Add remaining ingredients. Cover and simmer over low heat for 1½ hours or until meat is tender, or bake in 325° oven for 1½ hours. Remove bay leaf before serving. For 1 serving, refrigerate or freeze remaining half for another meal.

STIR-FRIED BEEF AND VEGETABLES

Serve this colorful blend of meat and vegetables with rice.

	FOR 1	FOR 2
beef steak, partially frozen for easy slicing	¼ lb.	½ lb.
soy sauce	1 tbs.	2 tbs.
sherry	1 tsp.	2 tsp.
oil	1 tsp.	2 tsp.
sugar	¼ tsp.	½ tsp.
ginger	dash	dash
oil	1 tbs.	2 tbs.
thinly sliced (on diagonal) carrot	¼ cup	½ cup
green onion, thinly sliced on diagonal	1	2
thinly sliced (on diagonal) green beans	½ cup	1 cup
thinly sliced mushrooms	½ cup	1 cup

Thinly slice steak. Combine soy sauce, sherry, oil, sugar and ginger. Pour over meat and set aside to marinate a few minutes. Heat 1 or 2 tbs. oil in a wok or frying pan. Add vegetables and stir-fry about 2 minutes until tender crisp. Remove from pan and set aside. Add meat to wok and stir-fry quickly, about 30 seconds. Return vegetables to pan, toss with meat and serve immediately.

VEAL PICCATA

This delicious veal dish, flavored with lemon and capers, is quick and easy.

	FOR 1	FOR 2
sliced veal	3 oz.	6 oz.
flour	1 tbs.	2 tbs.
salt and pepper		
butter	2 tsp.	4 tsp.
dry white wine	2 tbs.	¼ cup
capers	1 tsp.	2 tsp.
lemon juice	1 tsp.	2 tsp.

Pound veal slices to ¼-inch thickness. Season flour with salt and pepper and dredge meat in seasoned flour. Sauté veal in butter until lightly browned, 1 or 2 minutes per side. Remove to heated platter. Pour wine into frying pan and bring to a boil. Stir in capers and lemon juice. Pour sauce over veal and serve immediately.

MOCK RAVIOLI

Servings: 2

Or perhaps mock lazagna! Call it what you will, you will love it!

½ lb. ground beef
¼ cup chopped onion
½ clove garlic, minced
1 cup *Tomato Sauce*, page 30
dash oregano, basil, chili powder
  and sugar

½ cup sliced mushrooms
1 cup uncooked bow-tie pasta
2 cups chopped fresh spinach
1 egg, beaten
¼ cup grated Romano or Parmesan
  cheese

Brown ground beef and onion in a skillet over medium-high heat. Drain fat. Add garlic, *Tomato Sauce*, seasonings and mushrooms. Simmer 30 minutes. Cook pasta in boiling salted water 10 minutes. Drain well. Combine cooked pasta with spinach and egg. Spread half of meat sauce in a baking dish. Add half of pasta mixture. Spread remaining meat sauce over pasta and top with remaining pasta mixture. Sprinkle with cheese. Bake in a 350° oven for 30 minutes. For 1 serving, refrigerate or freeze half, either before or after baking, for another meal.

LAMB CHOPS RATATOUILLE

This delicious entrée goes together quickly.

	FOR 1	FOR 2
lamb chop, well trimmed	1	2
sliced zucchini	½ cup	1 cup
chopped eggplant	½ cup	1 cup
clove garlic, chopped	½	1
chopped onion	1 tbs.	2 tbs.
chopped tomato	¼ cup	½ cup
thyme	dash	dash
basil	dash	dash
salt and pepper		

Place lamb chop on a square of aluminum foil. Top with remaining ingredients. Bring ends of foil together and loosely fold to form package with opening at top to allow steam to escape. Bake in a 350° oven for 1 hour, or until meat is tender. If desired, meat and vegetables may be baked in a covered baking dish.

SWISS STEAK

Servings: 2

Meat braised in a savory vegetable sauce is marvelous with mashed potatoes.

½ lb. round steak
2 tbs. flour
salt and pepper
1 tbs. oil
1 small onion, sliced

1 cup sliced carrots
¼ cup chopped green bell pepper
1 cup *Tomato Sauce*, page 30
salt and pepper

Mix flour with salt and pepper. Pound into meat. Heat oil in a skillet over medium-high heat and brown meat. Remove to a baking dish and top with vegetables, *Tomato Sauce*, salt and pepper. Cover and bake in a 350° oven for 1 hour or until meat is tender. For 1 serving, refrigerate or freeze remaining half for another meal.

STEAK AU POIVRE

Complete your menu with **Garlic Potato Strips**, *page 103,* **Asparagus with Mustard Sauce**, *page 99, and* **Chocolate Mousse**, *page 156.*

	FOR 1	FOR 2
beef sirloin	6 oz.	12 oz.
coarsely ground black pepper	2 tbs.	1/4 cup
salt		
cognac	1 tbs.	2 tbs.
cream	1 tbs.	2 tbs.

Cut steak into serving pieces. Press pepper into meat. Sprinkle salt over bottom of a heavy skillet and place over high heat. When salt begins to brown, add steak and cook over high heat for several minutes. Turn steak, lower heat, and cook to desired doneness. Pour cognac over steak and ignite. When flames die, remove steak to a heated plate. Add cream to skillet and cook, stirring, until thickened. Pour sauce over steak.

ORANGE PORK CHOPS

Sweet potato and orange slices enhance the flavor of pork in this recipe.

	FOR 1	FOR 2
pork chop	1	2
oil	1½ tsp.	1 tbs.
sweet potato or yam, peeled	½	1
orange, sliced	¼	½
cinnamon dash dash		
salt and pepper		

Brown pork in hot oil. Cut sweet potato into ½-inch slices. Place meat and sweet potato slices in a baking dish and cover with orange slices. Bake covered in a 350° oven for 1 hour, or until meat is tender.

PORK CHOPS WITH BROWN RICE

This old favorite is especially tailored for 1 or 2.

	FOR 1	FOR 2
oil	1½ tsp.	1 tbs.
pork chop	1	2
beef broth	½ cup	1 cup
dry white wine	2 tbs.	¼ cup
carrot, cut into julienne strips	½	1
chopped onion	2 tbs.	¼ cup
marjoram	dash	dash
oregano	dash	dash
salt and pepper		
uncooked brown rice	¼ cup	½ cup

Heat oil in an oven-proof skillet over medium-high heat. Brown meat well, remove from pan and set aside. Drain excess fat from pan. Add broth, wine, carrot, onion and seasonings to pan and bring to a boil. Stir in rice and arrange pork chops over all. Remove from stovetop, cover and bake in a 350° oven for 1 hour or until liquid is absorbed.

SPARERIBS

Be prepared to eat these with your fingers!

	FOR 1	FOR 2
country-style spareribs	1 lb.	2 lb.
Barbecue Sauce, page 29	½ recipe	1 recipe

Place ribs in a roasting pan meat side up. Roast in a 450° oven for 25 minutes. Drain off all fat and pour sauce over ribs. Bake in a 350° oven for 1 hour or barbecue over medium coals for 30 to 40 minutes. Baste ribs occasionally and add water if sauce becomes too thick.

LAMB STEW

Servings: 2

This savory stew is real comfort food for a rainy winter evening.

½ lb. lamb for stew, cubed
  (1 lb. lamb shoulder chops)
1 cup chicken stock
¼ cup chopped onion
1 bay leaf
salt and pepper
dash of dill

1 potato, cubed
2 carrots, sliced
1 small rutabaga, peeled and cubed,
  or 1 cup shredded cabbage
2 tbs. water
1 tbs. flour

Combine lamb, stock and seasonings in a saucepan. Bring to a boil, reduce heat and simmer 1 hour. Add vegetables and simmer 30 minutes or until meat and vegetables are tender. Blend flour and water together to form a paste. Add to stew, stirring until thickened. Remove bay leaf before serving. For 1 serving, refrigerate or freeze remaining half for another meal.

SHISH KABOBS

Choose from lamb or beef and a variety of vegetables for a delicious, colorful meal.

	FOR 1	FOR 2
lamb or beef, cut into 1-inch cubes	⅓ lb.	⅔ lb.
LAMB MARINADE		
lemon juice	1 tbs.	2 tbs.
olive oil	2 tbs.	¼ cup
clove garlic, chopped	½	1
thyme	dash	dash
BEEF MARINADE		
red wine	1 tbs.	2 tbs.
olive oil	2 tbs.	¼ cup
garlic clove, chopped	½	1
bay leaf, crumbled	½	1

VEGETABLES

- mushrooms
- cherry tomatoes
- green, red or yellow bell pepper pieces
- pineapple chunks
- zucchini chunks
- eggplant cubes
- onion wedges

Trim fat from meat. Combine ingredients for desired marinade, add meat and marinate several hours or overnight in the refrigerator. Drain, reserving marinade. Select 2 or 3 vegetables and thread on skewers, alternating with meat. Broil 4 inches from heat for 8 minutes, or barbecue over hot coals for 10 minutes. Turn and baste with reserved marinade.

POULTRY

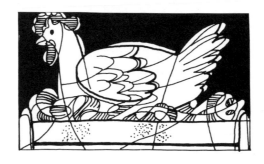

We usually recommend buying foods in single- or double-portion servings. However, when it comes to chicken, we suggest you buy a whole one. You can save money by cutting it up yourself. One chicken makes at least two meals for two people. The breast, thighs and legs can be made into a number of dishes: fried chicken, broiled chicken, barbecued chicken, etc. Leftovers from these dishes can be made into crepes, omelets, soups or sandwiches.

The wings, bones and skin can be made into chicken stock. Cover them with water and add a stalk of celery, a bay leaf and a few peppercorns. Simmer for about 2 hours. Strain liquid and discard seasonings. Place in the refrigerator overnight and discard hardened fat the next day. Use stock in other recipes or make it into soup by adding diced chicken, vegetables, rice or noodles.

For the cost of a chicken and a little work, just think of all the money you have saved!

OVEN FRIED CHICKEN

This chicken dish is traditionally served with hot biscuits and honey. A good take-along for a picnic, too.

	FOR 1	FOR 2
chicken pieces	3/4 lb.	1 1/2 lb.
bread crumbs or wheat germ	2 tbs.	1/4 cup
grated Parmesan cheese	2 tbs.	1/4 cup
paprika	1/8 tsp.	1/4 tsp.
salt	1/8 tsp.	1/4 tsp.
pepper		
buttermilk or melted butter	2 tbs.	1/4 cup

Wash chicken and dry with paper towels. Combine bread crumbs with cheese and seasonings. Dip chicken in buttermilk and then roll in crumb mixture. Place in a well-buttered baking dish. Bake in a 350° oven for 1 hour.

COQ AU VIN

This classic French dish features chicken cooked in red wine.

	FOR 1	FOR 2
oil	1 tsp.	2 tsp.
chopped onion	2 tbs.	1/4 cup
garlic clove, minced	1/2	1
chicken pieces	3/4 lb.	1 1/2 lb.
flour	1 1/2 tsp.	1 tbs.
minced parsley	1 1/2 tsp.	1 tbs.
bay leaf	1/4	1/2
thyme	pinch	1/8 tsp.
salt and pepper		
carrot, sliced	1/2	1
sliced fresh mushrooms	1/2 cup	1 cup
red wine	1 cup	2 cups

Place oil in a skillet over medium-high heat. Sauté onion and garlic. Add chicken and brown well on all sides. Sprinkle with flour and seasonings. Add carrot, mushrooms and wine. Cover and simmer 1 hour. Remove bay leaf.

GLAZED CHICKEN

*Baste the chicken with either the **Lemon-Herb Glaze** or the **Teriyaki Glaze**, each with its distinctive flavor. Use leftover chicken for **Chicken Sauce**, page 137, or **Chicken and Fruit Salad**, page 56.*

	FOR 1	**FOR 2**
chicken pieces	3/4 lb.	1½ lb.
salt and pepper		
Glaze, choose from recipes following		

Place chicken skin-side down on a baking or broiler pan. Sprinkle with salt and pepper and brush with desired glaze. Bake in a 375° oven for 20 minutes. Turn chicken and brush again with glaze. Bake 20 to 25 minutes longer, or until done. Or broil for 15 minutes, until lightly browned. Turn chicken, brush with glaze and broil 15 minutes longer, or until done.

LEMON-HERB GLAZE

	FOR 1	FOR 2
melted butter	1 tbs.	2 tbs.
lemon juice	1 tbs.	2 tbs.
tarragon or rosemary	¼ tsp.	½ tsp.

Mix together well.

TERIYAKI GLAZE

soy sauce	1 tbs.	2 tbs.
sherry	1 tbs.	2 tbs.
honey	1 tbs.	2 tbs.

Mix together well.

CHICKEN MORAGA

Serve with a tossed salad and pasta.

	FOR 1	FOR 2
chicken pieces	¾ lb.	1½ lb.
flour	2 tbs.	¼ cup
salt and pepper		
oil	1½ tsp.	1 tbs.
chopped onion	2 tbs.	¼ cup
sliced green bell pepper	2 tbs.	¼ cup
sliced fresh mushrooms	½ cup	1 cup
garlic clove, minced	½	1
Tomato Sauce, page 30	½ cup	1 cup
oregano	dash	dash

Place chicken in a plastic bag with flour, salt and pepper. Shake to coat. In a skillet over medium-high heat, brown chicken in oil. Remove from skillet and set aside. Sauté onion, green pepper, mushrooms and garlic in same skillet. Add chicken, *Tomato Sauce* and oregano. Cover and simmer 1 hour, or place in a baking dish and bake in a 350° oven for 1 hour.

GRILLED CHICKEN BREAST

Servings: 1-2

*Serve with **Armenian Rice**, page 91, or **Baked Noodles Ricotta**, page 89.*

1 or 2 chicken breast halves, boned
  and skinned

1 tbs. olive oil
salt and pepper

Preheat broiler or prepare grill. Place chicken halves between 2 pieces of waxed paper and pound until thin. Brush with olive oil and sprinkle with salt and pepper. Place chicken under broiler or on grill for 3 minutes. Turn chicken over and broil for 3 additional minutes.

VARIATIONS

- Instead of olive oil and seasonings, brush chicken with a mixture of 2 tbs. honey mixed with 1 tbs. Dijon mustard.

- For salt and pepper, substitute your favorite salt-free seasoning mix.

- Replace olive oil with Italian dressing.

- Instead of olive oil, sprinkle chicken with fresh lemon juice and dill.

CORNISH GAME HENS WITH ORANGE NUT STUFFING

This is the perfect choice for a company dinner.

	FOR 1	FOR 2
Rock Cornish game hen	1	2
melted butter	1 tbs.	2 tbs.
red currant jelly, melted	2 tbs.	¼ cup

Rinse hens and pat dry with paper towels. Stuff hens with *Orange Nut Stuffing*. Place breast-side up on a rack in a roasting pan. Brush with melted butter. Bake in a 350° oven for 1 hour or until legs more easily. Brush hens with jelly several times during the last 15 minutes of baking time to glaze.

ORANGE NUT STUFFING

	FOR 1	FOR 2
melted butter	1½ tsp.	1 tbs.
chopped onion	1½ tsp.	1 tbs.
long grain, brown or wild rice	¼ cup	½ cup
water	½ cup	1 cup
grated orange peel	1 tsp.	2 tsp.
chopped parsley	1½ tsp.	1 tbs.
chopped nuts	2 tbs.	¼ cup
poultry seasoning	dash	¼ tsp.
salt	dash	dash

Sauté onion in butter until tender. Add water and bring to a boil. Stir in remaining ingredients. Reduce heat to low, cover and cook until water is absorbed. Stuff hens.

STUFFED CHICKEN BREASTS

Cheese and herbs melt inside the tender chicken breast.

	FOR 1	FOR 2
chicken breast, skinned and boned	1 half	2 halves
salt and pepper		
soft butter	2 tbs.	¼ cup
oregano	dash	dash
chopped parsley	½ tsp.	1 tsp.
Monterey Jack or Swiss cheese	1 slice	2 slices
flour	2 tbs.	¼ cup
egg, beaten	1	1
bread crumbs or wheat germ	2 tbs.	¼ cup
dry white wine	2 tbs.	¼ cup

Pound chicken between 2 pieces of waxed paper until thin. Season with salt and pepper. Combine butter with herbs and spread mixture on chicken. Place slice of cheese on each piece of chicken and roll. Secure with a toothpick, if desired. Dip chicken in flour, egg and bread crumbs. Bake in a 375° oven for 15 minutes. Pour wine over chicken and bake 25 minutes longer.

CHICKEN SAUCE

Use this savory sauce served over rice, pasta or biscuits.

	FOR 1	FOR 2
butter	1 tbs.	2 tbs.
chopped onion	2 tbs.	¼ cup
sliced celery	2 tbs.	¼ cup
flour	1 tbs.	2 tbs.
chicken broth	¼ cup	½ cup
white wine	¼ cup	½ cup
salt and pepper		
tarragon or sage	⅛ tsp.	¼ tsp.
chopped parsley	1 tbs.	2 tbs.
cooked chicken or turkey, cubed	½ cup	1 cup

Sauté onion in butter until tender. Stir in flour. Add chicken broth and wine gradually, cooking and stirring until thickened. Add remaining ingredients. Heat through.

ROAST TURKEY BREAST
WITH CRANBERRY GLAZE

This recipe makes a holiday dinner for 1 or 2 with just enough leftovers for a couple of sandwiches.

1 turkey breast
salt
1 tbs. melted butter or oil
½ cup cranberry sauce
1 tbs. brown sugar
1 tsp. lemon juice

Place turkey on a rack in a roasting pan with skin side up. Sprinkle with salt and brush with melted butter. Roast in a 325° oven 25 minutes per pound, or until meat thermometer registers 170°. In a small bowl, combine cranberry sauce, brown sugar and lemon juice. During the last 15 minutes of roasting time, brush turkey several times with cranberry sauce mixture.

TURKEY CASSEROLE

Add this to your list of recipes for leftover chicken or turkey.

	FOR 1	FOR 2
butter	1½ tsp.	1 tbs.
flour	1½ tsp.	1 tbs.
chicken broth	¼ cup	½ cup
milk	¼ cup	½ cup
pepper	dash	dash
brown or wild rice	¼ cup	½ cup
diced cooked turkey or chicken	½ cup	1 cup
sliced fresh mushrooms	¼ cup	½ cup
chopped green bell pepper	1 tbs.	2 tbs.
sliced almonds	2 tbs.	¼ cup

Melt butter in a saucepan over medium-high heat. Add flour and blend. Stir in broth and milk. Cook, stirring, until thickened. Add remaining ingredients except almonds. Pour into a buttered baking dish and sprinkle with almonds. Cover and bake in a 350° oven for 1 hour or until rice is tender.

CHICKEN LIVERS IN PORT WINE

The flavors in this recipe blend to create a rich sauce. Serve with rice.

	FOR 1	FOR 2
minced onion	1 tbs.	2 tbs.
butter	1 tbs.	2 tbs.
chicken livers	¼ lb.	½ lb.
flour	1 tbs.	2 tbs.
chicken broth	¼ cup	½ cup
port wine	3 tbs.	6 tbs.
salt and pepper		
fresh or frozen peas	½ cup	1 cup

Sauté onion in butter over medium-high heat until tender. Add livers and cook 5 minutes, or until brown on all sides. Stir in flour. Add broth, port, salt and pepper and simmer 5 minutes. Add peas and cook 5 minutes longer. Serve over rice.

TURKEY TETRAZINNI

Servings: 2

This rich dish is said to be named for opera singer Luisa Tetrazzini.

2 tbs. butter
1½ cups sliced fresh mushrooms
¼ cup finely chopped green bell pepper
1½ tbs. flour
1 tsp. salt
dash pepper
1¼ cups half and half

2 cups diced cooked turkey or chicken
2 tbs. sherry
dash Tabasco Sauce
3 oz. uncooked spaghetti
1 egg yolk
1 tbs. grated Parmesan cheese, or to taste

Melt butter in a skillet over medium heat. Sauté mushrooms and pepper 5 minutes. Blend in flour, salt and pepper. Add cream, stirring constantly and cook until thickened. Add turkey and sherry; heat through. Season with Tabasco.

Cook spaghetti according to directions on page 84. Drain. Pour into a shallow, greased baking dish. Add a small amount of turkey mixture to egg yolk and stir thoroughly. Add remaining turkey mixture and stir until blended. Pour over spaghetti and sprinkle with cheese. Bake at 300° for 30 minutes. For 1 serving, refrigerate or freeze half and serve for another meal.

CHICKEN ZUCCHINI CASSEROLE

Serve with a tossed salad and one of our muffin variations.

	FOR 1	FOR 2
cooked rice	¼ cup	½ cup
chopped cooked chicken	¼ cup	½ cup
shredded Monterey Jack cheese	¼ cup	½ cup
zucchini, thinly sliced	6 slices	12 slices
tomato, thinly sliced	4 slices	8 slices
sour cream	¼ cup	½ cup
diced green chiles	1 tbs.	2 tbs.
oregano	⅛ tsp.	¼ tsp.
chopped green bell pepper	1 tbs.	2 tbs.
sliced green onion	1 tbs.	2 tbs.
salt and pepper		
grated Parmesan cheese		

Preheat oven to 350°. In a buttered casserole, layer rice, chicken, cheese, zucchini and tomato. Stir together sour cream, green chiles, oregano, green pepper, onion, salt and pepper. Pour over contents of casserole. Sprinkle with Parmesan cheese and bake uncovered for 30 minutes.

FISH AND SHELLFISH

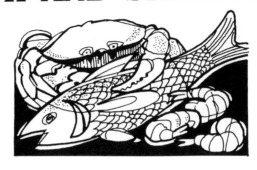

High in protein and low in fat, seafood is becoming increasingly popular throughout the country. Although it is at its peak when fresh, properly frozen seafood is a close second. If you are buying fresh fish, always choose ones that have no objectionable odor. Contrary to popular belief, fresh fish don't have an objectionable odor. Also, the flesh should spring back when touched with a finger and the scales adhere tightly to the skin. If a fish can't pass these tests, don't buy it; it isn't fresh.

If you get to the market and can't find the type of fish your recipe calls for, don't worry. Fortunately, almost any fish can be replaced with another of similar fat content, flavor and texture. Your fishmonger can help you determine this.

One more hint: don't overcook fish. Unlike many meats, fish is naturally tender. It need only be cooked until the flesh firms slightly and can be flaked with a fork. Serve it immediately after it is cooked.

SWORDFISH STEAKS

Swordfish retains its moisture when baked in foil.

	FOR 1	FOR 2
swordfish steak, approximately 8 oz.	1	2
dry vermouth	¼ cup	½ cup
salt and pepper		
lemon wedges		

Preheat oven to 375°. Place swordfish steak on a sheet of foil, curving the edges up. Pour vermouth over swordfish and season with salt and pepper. Seal edges of foil to enclose swordfish and place on a baking sheet. Bake for 10 minutes. Carefully remove from foil and serve with lemon wedges.

BAKED FISH

This easy recipe gives you a choice of two sauces.

	FOR 1	FOR 2
fish fillets	6 oz.	¾ lb.
salt and pepper		
Sauce, choose from recipes following		
lemon wedges		

Place fish in a buttered baking dish. Sprinkle with salt and pepper and top with the sauce of your choice. Bake in a 350° oven for 25 minutes, or until fish flakes easily when tested with a fork. Garnish with lemon wedges.

LEMON PARSLEY SAUCE

	FOR 1	FOR 2
melted butter	1 tbs.	2 tbs.
minced parsley	2 tsp.	4 tsp.
lemon juice	2 tsp.	4 tsp.

Mix ingredients together well.

DILL SOUR CREAM SAUCE

	FOR 1	FOR 2
sour cream	2 tbs.	¼ cup
chopped chives	½ tsp.	1 tsp.
dill	dash	dash

Mix ingredients together well.

SAUTÉED SCALLOPS

*Serve with **Bulghur Pilaff**, page 93, and a crisp green salad. For variety, substitute prawns for scallops, being careful to cook only until they turn pink.*

	FOR 1	FOR 2
scallops	1/4 cup	1/2 cup
salt and pepper		
butter	2 tsp.	4 tsp.
garlic clove, minced	1/2	1
white wine	2 tbs.	1/4 cup
chopped parsley	1 tsp.	2 tsp.
lemon wedges		

Rinse scallops and pat dry with paper towels. Melt butter in a skillet over medium-high heat. Add garlic and scallops and sauté until golden brown. Add wine and simmer 1 minute. Sprinkle with parsley and garnish with lemon wedges.

RED SNAPPER ALMONDINE

You may substitute fillet of sole for the red snapper in this recipe.

	FOR 1	FOR 2
red snapper fillets	6 oz.	¾ lb.
milk	1 tbs.	2 tbs.
bread crumbs	2 tbs.	¼ cup
salt and pepper		
butter	1 tbs.	2 tbs.
slivered almonds	1 tbs.	2 tbs.

Dip fillets in milk and then coat with bread crumbs which have been seasoned with salt and pepper. Melt butter in a skillet over medium-high heat. Sauté fillets in butter until golden brown and fish flakes easily when tested with a fork. Remove fish to a heated serving plate. Sauté almonds in pan drippings and spoon over fish.

SHRIMP RAMEKINS

You can prepare this ahead of time and pop it in the oven when you are ready to serve it.

	FOR 1	FOR 2
butter	1 tbs.	2 tbs.
flour	1 tbs.	2 tbs.
hot milk	1/3 cup	2/3 cup
chopped chives	1 tsp.	2 tsp.
cooked and deveined shrimp	1 cup	2 cups
sherry	1 tbs.	2 tbs.
salt and pepper		
bread crumbs or wheat germ	1 tsp.	2 tsp.
grated Parmesan cheese	1 tsp.	2 tsp.

Melt butter in a small saucepan over medium heat. Stir in flour until blended. Quickly stir in milk and cook, stirring, until thickened. Add chives, shrimp, sherry, salt and pepper. Spoon into buttered ramekins or baking shells. Sprinkle with bread crumbs and cheese. Bake in a 350° oven for 15 minutes.

SAVORY SALMON

*Serve with **Hollandaise Sauce**, page 26, for an elegant meal.*

	FOR 1	FOR 2
salmon steak	1	2
butter	1 tsp.	2 tsp.
salt and pepper		
dill	dash	dash
tarragon	dash	dash
capers	1 tsp.	2 tsp.

Place salmon in a buttered baking dish. Dot with butter and sprinkle with seasonings. Cover and bake in a 400° oven for 15 minutes, or until salmon flakes when tested with a fork.

STUFFED TROUT

Mushrooms and lemon enhance the delicate flavor of trout.

	FOR 1	FOR 2
trout	1 medium	2 medium
salt and pepper		
butter	1 tbs.	2 tbs.
chopped mushrooms	¼ cup	½ cup
lemon juice	½ tsp.	1 tsp.
chopped parsley	1 tsp.	2 tsp.

Sprinkle cavity of trout with salt and pepper and dot with butter. Combine mushrooms, lemon juice and parsley. Spoon into cavity. Place trout in a buttered baking dish and bake in a 375° oven for 20 minutes or until fish flakes easily when tested with a fork.

TUNA SAUCE

Spoon over freshly baked popovers or toast, and sprinkle with paprika.

	FOR 1	FOR 2
sour cream	1/4 cup	1/2 cup
Worcestershire sauce	1/4 tsp.	1/2 tsp.
minced onion	1/2 tsp.	1 tsp.
dash pepper		
6-7 oz. can tuna, drained	1/2 can	1 can
paprika	dash	dash
parsley		

Combine sour cream, Worcestershire sauce and onion in a small saucepan. Place over medium-high heat and stir until mixture is hot, but do not allow to boil. Flake tuna and add to sour cream mixture. Heat to serving temperature and spoon over toast. Dust with paprika and garnish with parsley. Serve immediately.

DESSERTS

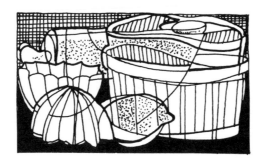

You could make an entire cake or pie, but how many pieces will you eat before it becomes stale? From some of our favorite last course selections, you can choose a dessert that will be just the right amount for you.

FRESH FRUIT FOR DESSERT

- Fresh fruits make an easy and nutritious finale to any meal. A basket of colorful fruits can serve as a centerpiece as well as dessert.

- Serve assorted fruits and cheeses with crackers, nuts and dates.

- Serve sliced fresh fruits topped with sour cream and brown sugar, sherbet, soft ice cream, whipped cream, yogurt and honey, frozen yogurt, granola, coconut, raisins, dates, sliced almonds or walnuts.

- Marinate sliced fresh fruit in wine for a few minutes.

- Dip fresh fruit in 6 oz. chocolate chips melted with ¼ cup evaporated milk — chocolate fondue.

- Combine ¼ cup sour cream with 1 tbs. brown sugar or honey and 1 tsp. lemon juice. Use as a dip for strawberries or grapes.

- Drizzle liqueur over fresh fruit: try orange liqueur over orange slices; amaretto over raspberries or other berries; cream de menthe over melon balls. Experiment with your favorite fruits and liqueurs.

CHOCOLATE MOUSSE

Serve this delicious dessert in your most glamorous stemware.

	FOR 1	FOR 2
semi-sweet chocolate	1 oz.	2 oz.
water	1 tbs.	2 tbs.
egg yolk	1	2
sugar	2 tbs.	¼ cup
egg white, beaten to stiff peaks	1	2

Heat chocolate and water in the top of a double boiler over barely simmering water or in a microwave until melted. Stir until blended and set aside to cool. Beat egg yolks and sugar until pale yellow and creamy. Beat in chocolate until well blended. Fold egg whites into chocolate mixture. Pour mousse into individual goblets or dessert dishes. Chill several hours or overnight.

GINGERBREAD

Servings: 9

Top with whipped cream and garnish with sliced fresh fruit. Freeze extra portions for future enjoyment.

½ cup butter or margarine
½ cup sugar
1 egg
2½ cups flour
1½ tsp. soda
½ tsp. salt

1 tsp. cinnamon
1 tsp. ginger
½ tsp. cloves
1 cup dark molasses
1 cup water

Preheat oven to 350°. Cream butter and sugar together; add egg and blend. Combine dry ingredients and mix into butter mixture alternately with molasses and water. Pour batter into a greased, floured 9x9x2-inch baking pan. Bake for 40 minutes or until done.

NUT BREAD WITH VARIATIONS

Makes: 1 loaf or 3 small loaves

Enjoy a slice of nut bread with a cup of tea. Nut breads freeze well.

2 cups flour
1 tbs. baking powder
½ tsp. salt
1 cup chopped walnuts, pecans or almonds
¾ cup sugar
1 cup milk
1 egg
¼ cup oil

Preheat oven to 350°. Stir together dry ingredients. Mix together milk, egg and oil. Add this mixture to the dry ingredients. Stir until just blended. Pour batter into a greased, floured 9x5x3-inch loaf pan or into 3 greased, floured small 6x3x2-inch loaf pans. Bake for 50 to 55 minutes for standard loaf or until bread tests done. Bake 3 small loaves for 45 minutes or until done. Cool in pan for about 5 minutes; remove from pan and continue cooling on a wire rack.

VARIATIONS

Add one of the following to the batter:

- ¾ cup chopped dates
- 1 cup mashed banana and reduce milk to ½ cup
- ½ cup chopped cranberries and 1 tbs. orange peel
- ¾ cup chopped dried apricots
- 1 tbs. grated lemon peel
- ½ cup raisins and ½ tsp. cinnamon
- ½ cup chocolate chips
- ¾ cup chopped dried pears
- ¾ cup chopped dried prunes

FRESH FRUIT SHERBET

Servings: 2

This dessert is refreshing on a warm summer's evening — or any evening!

1 cup fully ripened strawberries, blackberries, raspberries or peaches
¼ cup sugar, or more if fruit is tart
½ cup buttermilk
1 egg white, stiffly beaten

Puree fruit in a blender or food processor. Mix in sugar and let stand 10 minutes. Stir in buttermilk and fold in beaten egg white. Pour into ice cube trays or other freezer container and place in freezer. Stir sherbet gently every 2 hours until firm.

BAKED APPLES

Baked apples are delicious warm or cold — great for breakfast as well as for dessert. Serve with a dollop of yogurt or sweetened cream, either plain or whipped.

	FOR 1	FOR 2
baking apple	1	2
brown sugar	1 tbs.	2 tbs.
chopped walnuts	2 tsp.	1 tbs.
chopped dates or raisins	1 tbs.	2 tbs.
cinnamon	sprinkle	sprinkle
butter	1 tsp.	2 tsp.
cream or yogurt, optional		

Wash and core apples. Combine brown sugar, walnuts and dates. Fill apples with mixture, sprinkle with cinnamon and dot with butter. Place in a baking dish. Add water to just cover bottom of dish. Bake in a 350° oven for 45 minutes or until apples are tender.

BAKED APRICOTS

This is a different and delightful fruit dessert.

	FOR 1	FOR 2
apricots, pitted and halved	4	8
water	2 tbs.	¼ cup
brown sugar	2 tsp.	4 tsp.

Preheat oven to 350°. Place apricot halves in a small baking dish. Add water and sprinkle with brown sugar. Bake for 30 minutes or until apricots are soft. Serve warm or cold.

OUR FAVORITE BROWNIES

Makes: 16

Freeze these delicious brownies for instant treats.

1/4 cup butter

1/2 cup sugar

2 eggs

1 can (5.5 oz.) Hershey's chocolate syrup

1/2 cup flour

1/2 tsp. vanilla

dash salt

1/2 cup chopped nuts

Cream butter and sugar; add eggs and beat well. Add remaining ingredients and stir until blended. Pour batter into a greased and floured 8x8x2-inch baking pan. Bake in a 350° oven for 40 minutes. Cool and frost. When frosting is set, cut into squares.

FROSTING

1/2 cup sugar

3 tbs. milk

1/4 cup semi-sweet chocolate chips

Combine sugar and milk in a small saucepan. Boil for 5 minutes, or until mixture reaches soft ball stage, stirring occasionally. Add chocolate chips and stir until melted. Spread frosting over cooled brownies.

FRESH FRUIT TARTS

Take advantage of fruits in season for this delicious dessert.

SINGLE CRUST TARTS (makes 2)

½ cup flour
dash salt

3 tbs. butter or margarine
1 tbs. ice water

DOUBLE CRUST TARTS (makes 2)

¾ cup flour
¼ tsp. salt

4 tbs. butter or margarine
2 tbs. ice water

Combine flour and salt. Cut in butter until mixture resembles coarse cornmeal. Stir in water with a fork until dough holds together. Form 2 balls for single crust tarts or 4 balls for double crust tarts. Flatten balls, wrap in plastic and chill for 25 minutes.

For single crust tarts, roll pastry out on a floured surface into two 6½-inch rounds to fit 4½-inch tart pans. Fit pastry into pans and flute edges. Fill with fruit, sprinkle with *Crumb Topping*, page 166, and bake in a 400° oven for 30 to 40 minutes. For baked shells, prick pastry with a fork and bake unfilled in a 450° oven for 10 to 12 minutes, or until golden. Fill as desired.

For double crust tarts, roll pastry out on a floured surface into two 6½-inch rounds. Fit into 4½-inch tart pans. Roll remaining pastry into 2 rounds large enough to cover tops of tarts. Lay over filling. Flute edges, prick with a fork and sprinkle with sugar. Bake in a 400° oven for 30 to 40 minutes until crust is golden.

APPLE
2 cups apples
  peeled, cored,
  and sliced
¼ cup sugar
1 tbs. flour
  or tapioca
¼ tsp. cinnamon

APRICOT
1 cup apricots,
  pitted, sliced
⅓ cup sugar
1 tbs. flour
  or tapioca

BLACKBERRY
2 cups
  blackberries
¼ cup sugar
1 tbs. flour
  or tapioca

PEACH
2 cups peaches
  peeled, pitted
  and sliced
⅓ cup sugar
1 tbs. flour or
  tapioca
¼ tsp. cinnamon

Combine fruit with sugar, flour and spice. Spoon fruit mixture into prepared pastry shells. Sprinkle with *Crumb Topping*, or if making double crust tarts, top with pastry.

CRUMB TOPPING

1/4 cup flour
2 tbs. brown sugar
2 tbs. butter
2 tbs. rolled oats or chopped nuts, optional

Combine flour and sugar; cut in butter. Add rolled oats or nuts if desired. Sprinkle topping over single crust tarts. Bake in a 400° oven for 30 or 40 minutes.

FRUIT CRISP

Arrange fruit mixture in individual baking dishes without crust. Top with *Crumb Topping*. Bake in a 400° oven for 30 minutes.

INDEX

Serve Creative, Easy, Nutritious Meals with nitty gritty® Cookbooks

100 Dynamite Desserts
The 9 x 13 Pan Cookbook
The Barbecue Cookbook
Beer and Good Food
The Best Bagels are Made at Home
The Best Pizza is Made at Home
Bread Baking
Bread Machine Cookbook
Bread Machine Cookbook II
Bread Machine Cookbook III
Bread Machine Cookbook IV
Bread Machine Cookbook V
Bread Machine Cookbook VI
Cappuccino/Espresso
Casseroles
The Coffee Book
Convection Oven Cookery
Cooking for 1 or 2
Cooking in Clay
Cooking in Porcelain
Cooking on the Indoor Grill
Cooking with Chile Peppers
Cooking with Grains
Cooking with Your Kids

Creative Mexican Cooking
Deep Fried Indulgences
The Dehydrator Cookbook
Edible Pockets for Every Meal
Entrées From Your Bread Machine
Extra-Special Crockery Pot Recipes
Fabulous Fiber Cookery
Fondue and Hot Dips
Fresh Vegetables
From Freezer, 'Fridge and Pantry
From Your Ice Cream Maker
The Garlic Cookbook
Gourmet Gifts
Healthy Cooking on the Run
Healthy Snacks for Kids
The Juicer Book
The Juicer Book II
Lowfat American Favorites
Marinades
Muffins, Nut Breads and More
The New Blender Book
New International Fondue Cookbook
No Salt, No Sugar, No Fat
One-Dish Meals

The Pasta Machine Cookbook
Pinch of Time: Meals in Less than 30
    Minutes
Recipes for the Loaf Pan
Recipes for the Pressure Cooker
Recipes for Yogurt Cheese
Risottos, Paellas, and other Rice
    Specialties
Rotisserie Oven Cooking
The Sandwich Maker Cookbook
The Sensational Skillet: Sautés and
    Stir-Fries
Slow Cooking in Crock-Pot,® Slow
    Cooker, Oven and Multi-Cooker
The Steamer Cookbook
The Toaster Oven Cookbook
Unbeatable Chicken Recipes
The Vegetarian Slow Cooker
The Versatile Rice Cooker
Waffles
The Well Dressed Potato
Worldwide Sourdoughs from Your
    Bread Machine
Wraps and Roll-Ups

For a free catalog, call: Bristol Publishing Enterprises, Inc.
(800) 346-4889
www.bristolcookbooks.com